CW00531405

Contents

*The Complete
Nonsense Books*

A BOOK OF NONSENSE

There was an old Derry down Derry
Who loved to see little folks merry;
  So he made them a book,
  And with laughter they shook
At the fun of that Derry down Derry.

TO THE

GREAT-GRANDCHILDREN,

GRAND-NEPHEWS AND GRAND-NIECES

OF EDWARD, 13TH EARL OF DERBY,

THIS BOOK OF DRAWINGS AND VERSES

(THE GREATER PART OF WHICH WERE ORIGINALLY MADE
AND COMPOSED FOR THEIR PARENTS)

IS DEDICATED

BY THE AUTHOR,

EDWARD LEAR

LONDON, 1862

* 1.   There was an old man with a beard,
        Who said, "It is just as I feared!
            Two owls and a hen,
            Four larks and a wren,
        Have all built their nests in my beard!"

* 2.   There was a young lady of Ryde
        Whose shoestrings were seldom untied;
            She purchased some clogs
            And some small spotted dogs,
        And frequently walked about Ryde.

*3.   There was an old man with a nose,
       Who said, "If you choose to suppose
           That my nose is too long,
           You are certainly wrong!"
       That remarkable man with a nose.

*4.   There was an old man on a hill
       Who seldom, if ever, stood still;
           He ran up and down
           In his grandmother's gown,
       Which adorned that old man on a hill.

* 5.   There was a young lady whose bonnet
         Came untied when the birds sat upon it;
             But she said, "I don't care!
             All the birds in the air
         Are welcome to sit on my bonnet!"

* 6.   There was a young person of Smyrna
         Whose grandmother threatened to burn her;
             But she seized on the cat
             And said, "Granny, burn that!
         You incongruous old woman of Smyrna!"

*7.   There was an old person of Chile
      Whose conduct was painful and silly;
          He sat on the stairs,
          Eating apples and pears,
      That imprudent old person of Chile.

*8.   There was an old man with a gong,
      Who bumped at it all the day long;
          But they called out, "Oh, law!
          You're a horrid old bore!"
      So they smashed that old man with a gong.

*9.   There was an old lady of Chertsey
Who made a remarkable curtsy;
    She twirled round and round
    Till she sunk underground,
Which distressed all the people of Chertsey.

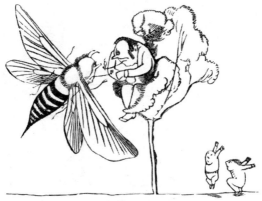

*10.   There was an old man in a tree
Who was horribly bored by a bee;
    When they said, "Does it buzz?"
    He replied, "Yes, it does!
It's a regular brute of a bee!"

* 11.   There was an old man with a flute –
      A sarpint ran into his boot;
        But he played day and night
        Till the sarpint took flight
      And avoided that man with a flute.

* 12.   There was a young lady whose chin
      Resembled the point of a pin;
        So she had it made sharp
        And purchased a harp,
      And played several tunes with her chin.

13. There was an old man of Kilkenny
    Who never had more than a penny;
        He spent all that money
        In onions and honey,
    That wayward old man of Kilkenny.

14. There was an old person of Ischia
    Whose conduct grew friskier and friskier;
        He danced hornpipes and jigs,
        And ate thousands of figs,
    That lively old person of Ischia.

* 15. There was an old man in a boat
        Who said, "I'm afloat, I'm afloat!"
            When they said, "No, you ain't!"
            He was ready to faint,
        That unhappy old man in a boat.

* 16. There was a young lady of Portugal
        Whose ideas were excessively nautical;
            She climbed up a tree
            To examine the sea,
        But declared she would never leave Portugal.

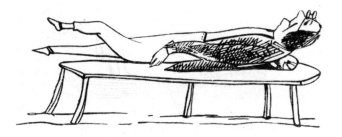

17. There was an old man of Moldavia
     Who had the most curious behaviour;
       For, while he was able,
       He slept on a table,
     That funny old man of Moldavia.

18. There was an old man of Madras
     Who rode on a cream-coloured ass;
       But the length of its ears
       So promoted his fears
     That it killed that old man of Madras.

* 19. There was an old person of Leeds
        Whose head was infested with beads;
           She sat on a stool
           And ate gooseberry fool,
        Which agreed with that person of Leeds.

20. There was an old man of Peru
     Who never knew what he should do;
        So he tore off his hair
        And behaved like a bear,
     That intrinsic old man of Peru.

21. There was an old person of Hurst
Who drank when he was not athirst;
 When they said, "You'll grow fatter"
 He answered, "What matter?"
That globular person of Hurst.

* 22. There was a young person of Crete
Whose toilette was far from complete;
 She dressed in a sack
 Spickle-speckled with black,
That ombliferous person of Crete.

23. There was an old man of the Isles
    Whose face was pervaded with smiles;
        He sung "High dum diddle"
        And played on the fiddle,
    That amiable man of the Isles.

24. There was an old person of Buda
    Whose conduct grew ruder and ruder,
        Till at last with a hammer
        They silenced his clamour
    By smashing that person of Buda.

25.   There was an old man of Columbia
Who was thirsty and called out for some beer;
    But they brought it quite hot
    In a small copper pot,
Which disgusted that man of Columbia.

26.   There was a young lady of Dorking
Who bought a large bonnet for walking;
    But its colour and size
    So bedazzled her eyes
That she very soon went back to Dorking.

* 27.   There was an old man who supposed
        That the street door was partially closed;
            But some very large rats
            Ate his coats and his hats
        While that futile old gentleman dozed.

28.   There was an old man of the West
      Who wore a pale plum-coloured vest;
          When they said, "Does it fit?"
          He replied, "Not a bit!"
      That uneasy old man of the West.

29.   There was an old man of the Wrekin
        Whose shoes made a horrible creaking,
            But they said, "Tell us whether
            Your shoes are of leather,
        Or of what, you old man of the Wrekin."

30.   There was a young lady whose eyes
        Were unique as to colour and size;
            When she opened them wide,
            People all turned aside
        And started away in surprise.

31. There was a young lady of Norway
     Who casually sat on a doorway;
         When the door squeezed her flat,
         She exclaimed, "What of that?"
     This courageous young lady of Norway.

32. There was an old man of Vienna
     Who lived upon tincture of senna;
         When that did not agree,
         He took camomile tea,
     That nasty old man of Vienna.

* 33.   There was an old person whose habits
          Induced him to feed upon rabbits;
              When he'd eaten eighteen,
              He turned perfectly green,
          Upon which he relinquished those habits.

* 34.   There was an old person of Dover
          Who rushed through a field of blue clover;
              But some very large bees
              Stung his nose and his knees,
          So he very soon went back to Dover.

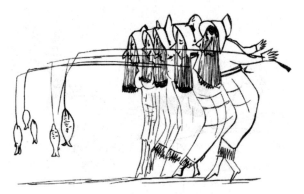

35.   There was an old man of Marseilles
      Whose daughters wore bottle-green veils;
         They caught several fish,
         Which they put in a dish
      And sent to their pa at Marseilles.

36.   There was an old person of Cadiz
      Who was always polite to all ladies;
         But in handing his daughter
         He fell into the water,
      Which drowned that old person of Cadiz.

* 37.   There was an old person of Basing
Whose presence of mind was amazing;
   He purchased a steed,
   Which he rode at full speed,
And escaped from the people of Basing.

38.   There was an old man of Quebec –
A beetle ran over his neck;
   But he cried, "With a needle
   I'll slay you, O beadle!"
That angry old man of Quebec.

* 39. There was an old person of Philae
       Whose conduct was dubious and wily;
          He rushed up a palm
          When the weather was calm,
       And observed all the ruins of Philae.

40. There was a young lady of Bute
    Who played on a silver-gilt flute;
       She played several jigs
       To her uncle's white pigs,
    That amusing young lady of Bute.

41.   There was a young lady whose nose
      Was so long that it reached to her toes;
        So she hired an old lady,
        Whose conduct was steady,
      To carry that wonderful nose.

42.   There was a young lady of Turkey,
      Who wept when the weather was murky;
        When the day turned out fine,
        She ceased to repine,
      That capricious young lady of Turkey.

43. There was an old man of Apulia
     Whose conduct was very peculiar;
         He fed twenty sons
         Upon nothing but buns,
     That whimsical man of Apulia.

* 44. There was an old man with a poker,
        Who painted his face with red ochre;
            When they said, "You're a guy!"
            He made no reply,
        But knocked them all down with his poker.

45.　There was an old person of Prague
　　　Who was suddenly seized with the plague;
　　　　But they gave him some butter,
　　　　Which caused him to mutter,
　　　And cured that old person of Prague.

46.　There was an old man of the North
　　　Who fell into a basin of broth;
　　　　But a laudable cook
　　　　Fished him out with a hook,
　　　Which saved that old man of the North.

47.   There was a young lady of Poole
        Whose soup was excessively cool;
           So she put it to boil
           By the aid of some oil,
        That ingenious young lady of Poole.

* 48.   There was an old person of Mold
        Who shrank from sensations of cold;
           So he purchased some muffs,
           Some furs and some fluffs,
        And wrapped himself up from the cold.

49.   There was an old man of Nepal
From his horse had a terrible fall;
    But, though split quite in two,
    By some very strong glue
They mended that man of Nepal.

50.   There was an old man of th' Abruzzi,
So blind that he couldn't his foot see;
    When they said, "That's your toe"
    He replied, "Is it so?"
That doubtful old man of th' Abruzzi.

51.   There was an old person of Rhodes
Who strongly objected to toads;
    He paid several cousins
    To catch them by dozens,
That futile old person of Rhodes.

52.   There was an old man of Peru
Who watched his wife making a stew;
    But once by mistake
    In a stove she did bake
That unfortunate man of Peru.

*53.   There was an old man of Melrose
            Who walked on the tips of his toes;
                But they said, "It ain't pleasant
                  To see you at present,
        You stupid old man of Melrose."

*54.   There was a young lady of Lucca
            Whose lovers completely forsook her;
                She ran up a tree
                And said, "Fiddle-de-dee!"
        Which embarrassed the people of Lucca.

55. There was an old man of Bohemia
     Whose daughter was christened Euphemia;
        Till one day, to his grief,
        She married a thief,
     Which grieved that old man of Bohemia.

56. There was an old man of Vesuvius
     Who studied the works of Vitruvius;
        When the flames burned his book,
        To drinking he took,
     That morbid old man of Vesuvius.

57. There was an old man of Cape Horn
Who wished he had never been born;
    So he sat on a chair
    Till he died of despair,
That dolorous man of Cape Horn.

58. There was an old lady whose folly
Induced her to sit in a holly;
    Whereupon, by a thorn
    Her dress being torn,
She quickly became melancholy.

59. There was an old man of Corfu
  Who never knew what he should do;
   So he rushed up and down
   Till the sun made him brown,
  That bewildered old man of Corfu.

60. There was an old man of the South
  Who had an immoderate mouth;
   But, in swallowing a dish
   That was quite full of fish,
  He was choked, that old man of the South.

61.   There was an old man of the Nile
        Who sharpened his nails with a file;
           Till he cut off his thumbs
           And said calmly, "This comes
        Of sharpening one's nails with a file!"

62.   There was an old person of Reims
        Who was troubled with horrible dreams;
           So, to keep him awake,
           They fed him with cake,
        Which amused that old person of Reims.

*63.　There was an old person of Cromer
　　　Who stood on one leg to read Homer;
　　　　　When he found he grew stiff,
　　　　　He jumped over the cliff,
　　　Which concluded that person of Cromer.

64.　There was an old person of Troy
　　　Whose drink was warm brandy and soy;
　　　　　Which he took with a spoon
　　　　　By the light of the moon,
　　　In sight of the city of Troy.

65. There was an old man of the Dee
Who was sadly annoyed by a flea;
　When he said, "I will scratch it"
　They gave him a hatchet,
Which grieved that old man of the Dee.

66. There was an old man of Dundee
Who frequented the top of a tree;
　When disturbed by the crows,
　He abruptly arose
And exclaimed, "I'll return to Dundee."

* 67. There was an old person of Tring
       Who embellished his nose with a ring;
           He gazed at the moon
           Every evening in June,
       That ecstatic old person of Tring.

* 68. There was an old man on some rocks
       Who shut his wife up in a box;
           When she said, "Let me out"
           He exclaimed, "Without doubt
       You will pass all your life in that box."

69.   There was an old man of Koblenz
       The length of whose legs was immense;
          He went with one prance
          From Turkey to France,
       That surprising old man of Koblenz.

70.   There was an old man of Calcutta
       Who perpetually ate bread and butter;
          Till a great bit of muffin,
          On which he was stuffing,
       Choked that horrid old man of Calcutta.

*71. There was an old man in a pew
Whose waistcoat was spotted with blue;
 But he tore it in pieces
 To give to his nieces,
That cheerful old man in a pew.

*72. There was an old man who said, "How
Shall I flee from this horrible cow?
 I will sit on this stile
 And continue to smile,
Which may soften the heart of that cow."

73. There was a young lady of Hull
Who was chased by a virulent bull;
But she seized on a spade
And called out, "Who's afraid?"
Which distracted that virulent bull.

*74. There was an old man of Whitehaven
Who danced a quadrille with a raven;
But they said, "It's absurd
To encourage this bird!"
So they smashed that old man of Whitehaven.

75.   There was an old man of Leghorn,
        The smallest as ever was born;
           But quickly snapped up he
           Was once by a puppy,
        Who devoured that old man of Leghorn.

76.   There was an old man of the Hague
        Whose ideas were excessively vague;
           He built a balloon
           To examine the moon,
        That deluded old man of the Hague.

77.   There was an old man of Jamaica
       Who suddenly married a Quaker;
           But she cried out, "Alack!
           I have married a black!"
       Which distressed that old man of Jamaica.

*78.   There was an old person of Dutton
       Whose head was so small as a button;
           So, to make it look big,
           He purchased a wig
       And rapidly rushed about Dutton.

79. There was a young lady of Tyre
Who swept the loud chords of a lyre;
At the sound of each sweep,
She enraptured the deep
And enchanted the city of Tyre.

*80. There was an old man who said, "Hush!
I perceive a young bird in this bush!"
When they said, "Is it small?"
He replied, "Not at all!
It is four times as big as the bush!"

81.   There was an old man of the East
      Who gave all his children a feast;
         But they all ate so much,
         And their conduct was such,
      That it killed that old man of the East.

82.   There was an old man of Kamchatka
      Who possessed a remarkably fat cur;
         His gait and his waddle
         Were held as a model
      To all the fat dogs in Kamchatka.

83. There was an old man of the coast
Who placidly sat on a post;
    But when it was cold,
    He relinquished his hold
And called for some hot buttered toast.

* 84. There was an old person of Bangor
Whose face was distorted with anger;
    He tore off his boots
    And subsisted on roots,
That irascible person of Bangor.

*85.   There was an old man with a beard,
        Who sat on a horse when he reared;
            But they said, "Never mind!
            You will fall off behind,
        You propitious old man with a beard!"

86.   There was an old man of the West
        Who never could get any rest;
            So they set him to spin
            On his nose and his chin,
        Which cured that old man of the West.

*87. There was an old person of Anerley
        Whose conduct was strange and unmannerly;
            He rushed down the Strand
            With a pig in each hand,
        But returned in the evening to Anerley.

88. There was a young lady of Troy
        Whom several large flies did annoy;
            Some she killed with a thump,
            Some she drowned at the pump,
        And some she took with her to Troy.

89.   There was an old man of Berlin
       Whose form was uncommonly thin;
          Till he once, by mistake,
          Was mixed up in a cake,
       So they baked that old man of Berlin.

*90.   There was an old person of Spain
       Who hated all trouble and pain;
          So he sat on a chair
          With his feet in the air,
       That umbrageous old person of Spain.

91. There was a young lady of Russia
    Who screamed so that no one could hush her;
        Her screams were extreme –
        No one heard such a scream
    As was screamed by that lady of Russia.

* 92. There was an old man who said, "Well!
    Will *nobody* answer this bell?
        I have pulled day and night
        Till my hair has grown white,
    But nobody answers this bell!"

93. There was a young lady of Wales
     Who caught a large fish without scales;
         When she lifted her hook,
         She exclaimed, "Only look!"
     That ecstatic young lady of Wales.

94. There was an old person of Cheadle
     Who was put in the stocks by the beadle
         For stealing some pigs,
         Some coats and some wigs,
     That horrible person of Cheadle.

95.   There was a young lady of Welling
      Whose praise all the world was a-telling;
         She played on the harp
         And caught several carp,
      That accomplished young lady of Welling.

96.   There was an old person of Tartary
      Who divided his jugular artery;
         But he screeched to his wife,
         And she said, "Oh, my life!
      Your death will be felt by all Tartary!"

97. There was an old person of Chester
Whom several small children did pester;
 They threw some large stones,
 Which broke most of his bones
And displeased that old person of Chester.

*98. There was an old man with an owl,
Who continued to bother and howl;
 He sat on a rail
 And imbibed bitter ale,
Which refreshed that old man and his owl.

99.   There was an old person of Gretna
        Who rushed down the crater of Etna;
           When they said, "Is it hot?"
           He replied, "No, it's not!"
        That mendacious old person of Gretna.

100.   There was a young lady of Sweden
        Who went by the slow train to Weedon;
           When they cried, "Weedon Station!"
           She made no observation,
        But thought she should go back to Sweden.

101.   There was a young girl of Majorca
       Whose aunt was a very fast walker;
          She walked seventy miles
          And leapt fifteen stiles,
       Which astonished that girl of Majorca.

102.   There was an old man of the Cape
       Who possessed a large Barbary ape;
          Till the ape one dark night
          Set the house all alight,
       Which burned that old man of the Cape.

103. There was an old lady of Prague
Whose language was horribly vague;
    When they said, "Are these caps?"
    She answered, "Perhaps!"
That oracular lady of Prague.

104. There was an old person of Sparta
Who had twenty-five sons and one daughter;
    He fed them on snails
    And weighed them in scales,
That wonderful person of Sparta.

* 105. There was an old man at a casement
        Who held up his hands in amazement;
            When they said, "Sir, you'll fall!"
            He replied, "Not at all!"
        That incipient old man at a casement.

106. There was an old person of Burton
      Whose answers were rather uncertain;
          When they said, "How d'ye do?"
          He replied, "Who are you?"
      That distressing old person of Burton.

107. There was an old person of Ems,
Who casually fell in the Thames;
And when he was found,
They said he was drowned,
That unlucky old person of Ems.

* 108. There was an old person of Ewell,
Who chiefly subsisted on gruel;
But to make it more nice
He inserted some mice,
Which refreshed that old person of Ewell.

109. There was a young lady of Parma
      Whose conduct grew calmer and calmer;
          When they said, "Are you dumb?"
          She merely said, "Hum!"
      That provoking young lady of Parma.

*110. There was an old man of Aosta
       Who possessed a large cow, but he lost her;
           But they said, "Don't you see
           She has rushed up a tree?
       You invidious old man of Aosta!"

*111. There was an old man on whose nose
      Most birds of the air could repose;
         But they all flew away
         At the closing of day,
      Which relieved that old man and his nose.

112. There was a young lady of Clare
     Who was sadly pursued by a bear;
        When she found she was tired,
        She abruptly expired,
     That unfortunate lady of Clare.

113.   There was an old man of New York
       Who murdered himself with a fork;
           But nobody cried –
           Though he very soon died –
       For that silly old man of New York.

114.   There was an old sailor of Compton
       Whose vessel a rock it once bumped on;
           The shock was so great
           That it damaged the pate
       Of that singular sailor of Compton.

115. There was an old man of Kildare
   Who climbed into a very high chair;
      When he said, "Here I stays
      Till the end of my days"
   That immovable man of Kildare.

NONSENSE SONGS
AND STORIES

NONSENSE SONGS

THE OWL
AND
THE PUSSY CAT

I

The Owl and the Pussy Cat went to sea
   In a beautiful pea-green boat:
They took some honey, and plenty of money,
   Wrapped up in a five-pound note.
The Owl looked up to the stars above
   And sang to a small guitar,
"O lovely Pussy, O Pussy, my love,
   What a beautiful Pussy you are,
         You are,
         You are!
What a beautiful Pussy you are!"

II

Pussy said to the Owl, "You elegant fowl,
   How charmingly sweet you sing!
Oh, let us be married! Too long we have tarried –
   But what shall we do for a ring?"
They sailèd away, for a year and a day,
   To the land where the bong tree grows;
And there in a wood a Piggy-wig stood,
   With a ring at the end of his nose,
         His nose,
         His nose,
   With a ring at the end of his nose.

III

"Dear Pig, are you willing to sell for one shilling
   Your ring?" Said the Piggy, "I will."
So they took it away, and were married next day
   By the Turkey who lives on the hill.
They dinèd on mince and slices of quince,
   Which they ate with a runcible spoon;
And hand in hand, on the edge of the sand,
   They danced by the light of the moon,
         The moon,
         The moon,
   They danced by the light of the moon.

THE DUCK

AND

THE KANGAROO

I

Said the Duck to the Kangaroo,
  "Good gracious, how you hop
Over the fields, and the water too,
  As if you never would stop!
My life is a bore in this nasty pond,
And I long to go out in the world beyond:
  I wish I could hop like you,"
  Said the Duck to the Kangaroo.

II

"Please give me a ride on your back,"
  Said the Duck to the Kangaroo.
"I would sit quite still and say nothing but 'Quack'
  The whole of the long day through –
And we'd go to the Dee, and the Jelly Bo Lee,
Over the land, and over the sea.
  Please take me a ride! Oh, do!"
  Said the Duck to the Kangaroo.

III

Said the Kangaroo to the Duck,
   "This requires some little reflection.
Perhaps, on the whole, it might bring me luck,
   And there seems but one objection –
Which is, if you'll let me speak so bold,
Your feet are unpleasantly wet and cold,
   And would probably give me the roo-
   Matiz," said the Kangaroo.

IV

Said the Duck, "As I sat on the rocks,
   I have thought over that completely,
And I bought four pairs of worsted socks,
   Which fit my web feet neatly;
And to keep out the cold I've bought a cloak,
And every day a cigar I'll smoke –
   All to follow my own dear true
   Love of a Kangaroo!"

V

Said the Kangaroo, "I'm ready!
   All in the moonlight pale –
But to balance me well, dear Duck, sit steady,
   And quite at the end of my tail!"
So away they went with a hop and a bound,
And they hopped the whole world three times round.
   And who so happy – oh, who –
   As the Duck and the Kangaroo?

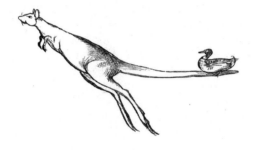

THE DADDY-LONG-LEGS

AND

THE FLY

I

Once Mr Daddy-Long-Legs,
  Dressed in brown and grey,
Walked about upon the sands
  Upon a summer's day –
And there among the pebbles,
  When the wind was rather cold,
He met with Mr Floppy Fly,
  All dressed in blue and gold;
And, as it was too soon to dine,
They drank some periwinkle wine,
And played an hour or two, or more,
At battlecock and shuttledore.

II

Said Mr Daddy-Long-Legs
    To Mr Floppy Fly,
"Why do you never come to court?
    I wish you'd tell me why.
All gold and shine, in dress so fine,
    You'd quite delight the court.
Why do you never go at all?
    I really think you *ought*!
And if you went, you'd see such sights!
Such rugs and jugs and candlelights!
And, more than all, the king and queen –
One in red, and one in green."

III

"Oh, Mr Daddy-Long-Legs,"
    Said Mr Floppy Fly,
"It's true I never go to court –
    And I will tell you why.
If I had six long legs like yours,
    At once I'd go to court!
But oh! I can't, because *my* legs
    Are so extremely short.
And I'm afraid the king and queen
(One in red, and one in green)
Would say aloud, 'You are not fit,
You Fly, to come to court a bit!'"

IV

"Oh, Mr Daddy-Long-Legs,"
    Said Mr Floppy Fly,
"I wish you'd sing one little song,
    One mumbian melody!
You used to sing so awful well
    In former days gone by;
But now you never sing at all –

I wish you'd tell me why.
For if you would, the silvery sound
Would please the shrimps and cockles round,
And all the crabs would gladly come
To hear you sing, 'Ah, Hum di Hum!'"

V

Said Mr Daddy-Long-Legs,
  "I can never sing again;
And, if you wish, I'll tell you why,
  Although it gives me pain.
For years I cannot hum a bit,
  Or sing the smallest song –
And this the dreadful reason is:
  My legs are grown too long!
My six long legs, all here and there,
Oppress my bosom with despair;
And if I stand or lie or sit,
I cannot sing one single bit!"

VI

So Mr Daddy-Long-Legs
  And Mr Floppy Fly
Sat down in silence by the sea
  And gazed upon the sky.
They said, "This is a dreadful thing!
  The world has all gone wrong,
Since one has legs too short by half,
  The other much too long!
One never more can go to court,
Because his legs have grown too short;
The other cannot sing a song,
Because his legs have grown too long!"

VII

Then Mr Daddy-Long-Legs
  And Mr Floppy Fly
Rushed downward to the foamy sea
  With one sponge-taneous cry –
And there they found a little boat,
  Whose sails were pink and grey;
And off they sailed among the waves,
  Far and far away.
They sailed across the silent main,
And reached the great Gromboolian Plain;
And there they play for evermore
At battlecock and shuttledore.

THE JUMBLIES

I

They went to sea in a sieve, they did –
  In a sieve they went to sea:
In spite of all their friends could say,
On a winter's morn, on a stormy day,
  In a sieve they went to sea!
And when the sieve turned round and round,
And every one cried, "You'll all be drowned!"
They called aloud, "Our sieve ain't big,
But we don't care a button, we don't care a fig!
  In a sieve we'll go to sea!"
      Far and few, far and few,
        Are the lands where the Jumblies live;
        Their heads are green, and their hands are blue,
        And they went to sea in a sieve.

II

They sailed away in a sieve, they did –
   In a sieve they sailed so fast,
With only a beautiful pea-green veil
Tied with a ribbon, by way of a sail,
   To a small tobacco-pipe mast.
And everyone said who saw them go,
"Oh, won't they be soon upset, you know!
For the sky is dark, and the voyage is long –
And happen what may, it's extremely wrong
   In a sieve to sail so fast!"
      Far and few, far and few,
        Are the lands where the Jumblies live;
        Their heads are green, and their hands are blue,
        And they went to sea in a sieve.

III

The water, it soon came in, it did –
   The water, it soon came in:
So to keep them dry, they wrapped their feet
In a pinky paper all folded neat,
   And they fastened it down with a pin.
And they passed the night in a crockery jar,
And each of them said, "How wise we are!
Though the sky be dark, and the voyage be long,
Yet we never can think we were rash or wrong,
   While round in our sieve we spin!"
      Far and few, far and few,
        Are the lands where the Jumblies live;
        Their heads are green, and their hands are blue,
        And they went to sea in a sieve.

IV

And all night long they sailed away –
  And when the sun went down,
They whistled and warbled a moony song
To the echoing sound of a coppery gong,
  In the shade of the mountains brown.
"O Timballo! How happy we are,
When we live in a sieve and a crockery jar!
And all night long in the moonlight pale,
We sail away with a pea-green sail
  In the shade of the mountains brown."
        Far and few, far and few,
          Are the lands where the Jumblies live;
          Their heads are green, and their hands are blue,
            And they went to sea in a sieve.

V

They sailed to the Western Sea, they did –
  To a land all covered with trees;
And they bought an owl, and a useful cart,
And a pound of rice, and a cranberry tart,
  And a hive of silvery bees;
And they bought a pig, and some green jackdaws,
And a lovely monkey with lollipop paws,
And forty bottles of ring-bo-ree,
  And no end of Stilton cheese.
        Far and few, far and few,
          Are the lands where the Jumblies live;
          Their heads are green, and their hands are blue,
            And they went to sea in a sieve.

VI

And in twenty years they all came back –
    In twenty years or more;
And everyone said, "How tall they've grown!
For they've been to the Lakes, and the Terrible Zone,
    And the hills of the Chankly Bore."
And they drank their health, and gave them a feast
Of dumplings made of beautiful yeast;
And everyone said, "If we only live,
We too will go to sea in a sieve,
    To the hills of the Chankly Bore."
        Far and few, far and few,
            Are the lands where the Jumblies live;
            Their heads are green, and their hands are blue,
                And they went to sea in a sieve.

THE NUTCRACKERS

AND

THE SUGAR-TONGS

I

The Nutcrackers sat by a plate on the table,
  The Sugar-Tongs sat by a plate at his side,
And the Nutcrackers said, "Don't you wish we were able
  Along the blue hills and green meadows to ride?
Must we drag on this stupid existence for ever,
  So idle and weary, so full of remorse,
While everyone else takes his pleasure, and never
  Seems happy unless he is riding a horse?

II

"Don't you think we could ride without being instructed,
  Without any saddle or bridle or spur?
Our legs are so long, and so aptly constructed,
  I'm sure that an accident could not occur.
Let us all of a sudden hop down from the table
  And hustle downstairs, and each jump on a horse!
Shall we try? Shall we go? Do you think we are able?"
  The Sugar-Tongs answered distinctly, "Of course!"

III

So down the long staircase they hopped in a minute;
    The Sugar-Tongs snapped, and the Crackers said, "Crack!"
The stable was open; the horses were in it:
    Each took out a pony and jumped on his back.
The Cat in a fright scrambled out of the doorway;
    The Mice tumbled out of a bundle of hay;
The brown and white Rats, and the black ones from Norway,
    Screamed out, "They are taking the horses away!"

IV

The whole of the household was filled with amazement:
    The Cups and the Saucers danced madly about;
The Plates and the Dishes looked out of the casement;
    The Salt Cellar stood on his head with a shout;
The Spoons, with a clatter, looked out of the lattice;
    The Mustard Pot climbed up the gooseberry pies;
The Soup Ladle peeped through a heap of veal patties
    And squeaked with a ladle-like scream of surprise.

V

The Frying Pan said, "It's an awful delusion!"
    The Tea Kettle hissed and grew black in the face;
And they all rushed downstairs in the wildest confusion
    To see the great Nutcracker–Sugar-Tong race.
And out of the stable, with screamings and laughter
    (Their ponies were cream-coloured, speckled with brown),
The Nutcrackers first, and the Sugar-Tongs after,
    Rode all round the yard, and then all round the town.

VI

They rode through the street, and they rode by the station;
    They galloped away to the beautiful shore;
In silence they rode, and "made no observation"
    Save this: "We will never go back any more!"
And still you might hear, till they rode out of hearing,
    The Sugar-Tongs snap and the Crackers say "Crack!" –
Till, far in the distance their forms disappearing,
    They faded away, and they never came back!

CALICO PIE

I

Calico pie,
The little Birds fly
Down to the calico tree;
Their wings were blue,
And they sang "Tilly-loo!"
Till away they flew —

And they never came back to me!
They never came back,
They never came back,
They never came back to me!

II

Calico jam,
The little Fish swam
Over the Syllabub Sea.
He took off his hat
To the Sole and the Sprat,
And the Willeby-wat –

But he never came back to me!
He never came back,
He never came back,
He never came back to me!

III

Calico ban,
The little Mice ran
To be ready in time for tea;
Flippity flup,
They drank it all up,
And danced in the cup –

But they never came back to me!
They never came back,
They never came back,
They never came back to me!

IV

Calico drum,
The Grasshoppers come,
The Butterfly, Beetle and Bee,
Over the ground,
Around and round,
With a hop and a bound –

But they never came back!
They never came back,
They never came back,
They never came back to me!

MR AND MRS SPIKKY SPARROW

I

On a little piece of wood
Mr Spikky Sparrow stood;
Mrs Sparrow sat close by,
A-making of an insect pie
For her little children five,
In the nest and all alive –
Singing with a cheerful smile
To amuse them all the while,
    "Twikky wikky wikky wee,
    Wikky bikky twikky tee,
      Spikky bikky bee!"

II

Mrs Spikky Sparrow said,
"Spikky, darling! In my head
Many thoughts of trouble come,
Like to flies upon a plum!
All last night, among the trees,
I heard you cough, I heard you sneeze;
And thought I, 'It's come to that

Because he does not wear a hat!'
Chippy wippy sikky tee,
Bikky wikky tikky mee,
Spikky chippy wee!

III

"Not that you are growing old –
But the nights are growing cold.
No one stays out all night long
Without a hat: I'm sure it's wrong!"
Mr Spikky said, "How kind,
Dear, you are, to speak your mind!
All your life I wish you luck!
You are, you are, a lovely duck!
Witchy witchy witchy wee,
Twitchy witchy witchy bee,
Tikky tikky tee!

IV

"I was also sad, and thinking,
When one day I saw you winking,
And I heard you sniffle-snuffle,
And I saw your feathers ruffle.
To myself I sadly said,
'She's neuralgia in her head!
That dear head has nothing on it!
Ought she not to wear a bonnet?'
Witchy kitchy kitchy wee,
Spikky wikky mikky bee,
Chippy wippy chee!

V

"Let us both fly up to town:
There I'll buy you such a gown!
Which, completely in the fashion,
You shall tie a sky-blue sash on;
And a pair of slippers neat
To fit your darling little feet,
So that you will look and feel

Quite galloobious and genteel.
    Jikky wikky bikky see,
    Chicky bikky wikky bee,
        Twicky witchy wee!"

VI

So they both to London went,
Alighting on the Monument;
Whence they flew down swiftly – pop! –
Into Moses' wholesale shop:
There they bought a hat and bonnet,
And a gown with spots upon it,
A satin sash of Cloxam blue,
And a pair of slippers too.
    Zikky wikky mikky bee,
    Witchy witchy mitchy kee,
        Sikky tikky wee!

VII

Then, when so completely dressed,
Back they flew, and reached their nest.
Their children cried, "O Ma and Pa!
How truly beautiful you are!"
Said they, "We trust that cold or pain
We shall never feel again –
While, perched on tree or house or steeple,
We now shall look like other people.
    Witchy witchy witchy wee,
    Twikky mikky bikky bee,
        Zikky sikky tee!"

THE BROOM, THE SHOVEL,
THE POKER
AND THE TONGS

I

The Broom and the Shovel, the Poker and Tongs,
   They all took a drive in the park;
And they each sang a song – ding-a-dong, ding-a-dong! –
   Before they went back in the dark.
Mr Poker, he sat quite upright in the coach;
   Mr Tongs made a clatter and clash;
Miss Shovel was dressed all in black (with a brooch);
   Mrs Broom was in blue (with a sash).
        Ding-a-dong, ding-a-dong!
        And they all sang a song!

II

"O Shovely so lovely!" the Poker, he sang,
   "You have perfectly conquered my heart.
Ding-a-dong, ding-a-dong! If you're pleased with my song,
   I will feed you with cold apple tart.

When you scrape up the coals with a delicate sound,
    You enrapture my life with delight!
Your nose is so shiny, your head is so round,
    And your shape is so slender and bright!
            Ding-a-dong, ding-a-dong!
            Ain't you pleased with my song?"

III

"Alas! Mrs Broom," sighed the Tongs in his song,
    "Oh, is it because I'm so thin,
And my legs are so long – ding-a-dong, ding-a-dong! –
    That you don't care about me a pin?
Ah, fairest of creatures, when sweeping the room,
    Ah, why don't you heed my complaint?
Must you needs be so cruel, you beautiful Broom,
    Because you are covered with paint?
            Ding-a-dong, ding-a-dong!
            You are certainly wrong!"

IV

Mrs Broom and Miss Shovel together they sang,
    "What nonsense you're singing today!"
Said the Shovel, "I'll certainly hit you a bang!"
    Said the Broom, "And I'll sweep you away!"
So the Coachman drove homeward as fast as he could,
    Perceiving their anger with pain;
But they put on the kettle, and little by little
    They all became happy again.
            Ding-a-dong, ding-a-dong!
            There's an end of my song!

THE TABLE AND THE CHAIR

I

Said the Table to the Chair,
"You can hardly be aware
How I suffer from the heat
And from chilblains on my feet!
If we took a little walk,
We might have a little talk;
Pray, let us take the air,"
Said the Table to the Chair.

II

Said the Chair unto the Table,
"Now, you *know* we are not able!
How foolishly you talk,
When you know we *cannot* walk!"
Said the Table with a sigh,
"It can do no harm to try.
I've as many legs as you:
Why can't we walk on two?"

III

So they both went slowly down
And walked about the town

With a cheerful bumpy sound
As they toddled round and round –
And everybody cried,
As they hastened to their side,
"See, the Table and the Chair
Have come out to take the air!"

IV

But in going down an alley,
To a castle in a valley,
They completely lost their way
And wandered all the day –
Till, to see them safely back,
They paid a Ducky-Quack,
And a Beetle and a Mouse,
Who took them to their house.

V

Then they whispered to each other,
"O delightful little brother,
What a lovely walk we've taken!
Let us dine on beans and bacon."
So the Ducky and the leetle
Browny-Mousy and the Beetle
Dined, and danced upon their heads
Till they toddled to their beds.

NONSENSE STORIES

THE STORY OF
THE FOUR LITTLE CHILDREN
WHO WENT ROUND THE WORLD

Once upon a time, a long while ago, there were four little people whose names were

VIOLET,   SLINGSBY,   GUY   and LIONEL;

and they all thought they should like to see the world. So they bought a large boat to sail quite round the world by sea, and then they were to come back on the other side by land. The boat was painted blue with green spots, and the sail was yellow with red stripes; and, when they set off, they only took a small Cat to steer and look after the boat, besides an elderly Quangle-Wangle, who had to cook the dinner and make the tea – for which purposes they took a large kettle.

For the first ten days they sailed on beautifully, and found plenty to eat, as there were lots of fish; and they had only to take them out of the sea with a long spoon, when the Quangle-Wangle instantly cooked them; and the Pussy Cat was fed with the bones, with which she expressed herself pleased, on the whole: so that all the party were very happy.

During the daytime, Violet chiefly occupied herself in putting salt water into a churn, while her three brothers churned it violently, in the hope that it would turn into butter, which it seldom if ever did; and in the evening they all retired into the tea kettle, where they all managed to sleep very comfortably, while Pussy and the Quangle-Wangle managed the boat.

After a time, they saw some land at a distance – and, when they came to it, they found it was an island made of water quite surrounded by earth. Besides that, it was bordered by evanescent isthmuses, with a great gulf stream running about all over it; so that it was perfectly beautiful, and contained only a single tree, 503 feet high.

When they had landed, they walked about, but found, to their great surprise, that the island was quite full of veal cutlets and chocolate drops, and nothing else. So they all climbed up the single high tree to discover, if possible, if there were any people; but, having remained on the top of the tree for a week and not seeing anybody, they naturally concluded that there were no inhabitants; and accordingly, when they came down, they loaded the boat with two thousand veal cutlets and a million of chocolate drops; and these afforded them sustenance for more than a month, during which time they pursued their voyage with the utmost delight and apathy.

After this, they came to a shore where there were no less than sixty-five great red parrots with blue tails, sitting on a rail all of a row, and all fast asleep. And I am sorry to say that the Pussy Cat and the Quangle-Wangle crept softly and bit off the tail feathers of all the sixty-five parrots; for which Violet reproved them both severely.

Notwithstanding which, she proceeded to insert all the feathers – two hundred and sixty in number – in her bonnet, thereby causing it to have a lovely and glittering appearance, highly prepossessing and efficacious.

The next thing that happened to them was in a narrow part of the sea, which was so entirely full of fishes that the boat could go on no further; so they remained there about six weeks, till they had eaten nearly all the fishes, which were soles, and all ready-cooked, and covered with shrimp sauce, so that there was no trouble whatever. And as the few fishes who remained uneaten complained of the cold, as well as of the difficulty they had in getting any sleep on account of the extreme noise made by the arctic bears and the tropical turnspits, which frequented the neighbourhood in great numbers, Violet most amiably knitted a small woollen frock for several of the fishes, and Slingsby administered some opium drops to them; through which kindness they became quite warm, and slept soundly.

Then they came to a country which was wholly covered with immense orange trees of a vast size, and quite full of fruit. So they all landed, taking with them the tea kettle, intending to gather some of the oranges and place them in it. But, while they were busy about this, a most dreadfully high wind rose, and blew out most the parrot-tail feathers from Violet's bonnet. That, however, was nothing compared with the calamity of the oranges falling down on their heads by millions and millions, which thumped and bumped and bumped and thumped them all so seriously that they were obliged to run as hard as they could for their lives; besides that, the sound of the oranges rattling on the tea kettle was of the most fearful and amazing nature.

Nevertheless, they got safely to the boat, although considerably vexed and hurt; and the Quangle-Wangle's right foot was so knocked about that he had to sit with his head in his slipper for at least a week.

This event made them all for a time rather melancholy; and perhaps they might never have become less so, had not Lionel, with a most praiseworthy devotion and perseverance, continued to stand on one leg and whistle to them in a loud and lively manner; which diverted the whole party so extremely that they gradually recovered their spirits and agreed that whenever they should reach home, they would subscribe towards a testimonial to Lionel, entirely made of gingerbread and raspberries, as an earnest token of their sincere and grateful infection.

After sailing on calmly for several more days, they came to another country, where they were much pleased and surprised to see a countless multitude of white Mice with red eyes, all sitting in a great circle, slowly eating custard pudding with the most satisfactory and polite demeanour.

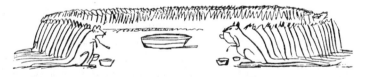

And as the four travellers were rather hungry, being tired of eating nothing but soles and oranges for so long a period, they held a council as to the propriety of asking the Mice for some of their pudding in a humble and affecting manner, by which they could hardly be otherwise than gratified. It was agreed, therefore, that Guy should go and ask the Mice, which he immediately did – and the result was that they gave a walnut shell only half full of custard diluted with water. Now, this displeased Guy, who said, "Out of such a lot of pudding as you have got, I must say, you might have spared a somewhat larger quantity". But no sooner had he finished speaking than the Mice turned round at once and sneezed at him in an appalling and vindictive manner (and it is impossible to imagine a more scroobious and unpleasant sound than that caused by the simultaneous sneezing of many millions of angry Mice); so that Guy rushed back to the boat, having first shied his cap into the middle of the custard pudding, by which means he completely spoiled the Mice's dinner.

By and by the four children came to a country where there were no houses, but only an incredibly innumerable number of large bottles without corks and of a dazzling and sweetly susceptible blue colour. Each of these blue bottles contained a Bluebottle Fly; and all these interesting animals live continually together in the most copious and rural harmony – nor perhaps in many parts of the world is such perfect and abject happiness to be found. Violet and Slingsby and Guy and Lionel were greatly struck with this singular and instructive settlement; and, having previously asked permission of the Bluebottle flies (which was most courteously granted), the boat was drawn up to the shore, and they proceeded to make tea in front of the bottles; but as they had no tea leaves, they merely placed some pebbles in the hot water; and the Quangle-Wangle played some tunes over it on an accordion, by which, of course, tea was made directly, and of the very best quality.

The four children then entered into conversation with the Bluebottle flies, who discoursed in a placid and genteel manner, though with a slightly buzzing accent, chiefly owing to the fact that they each held a small clothes brush between their teeth, which naturally occasioned a fizzy, extraneous utterance.

"Why," said Violet, "would you kindly inform us, do you reside in bottles – and, if in bottles at all, why not, rather, in green or purple, or, indeed, in yellow bottles?"

To which questions a very aged Bluebottle Fly answered: "We found the bottles here all ready to live in – that is to say, our great-great-great-great-great-grandfathers did: so we occupied them at once. And, when the winter comes on, we turn the bottles upside down, and consequently rarely feel the cold at all; and you know very well that this could not be the case with bottles of any other colour than blue."

"Of course it could not," said Slingsby. " But, if we may take the liberty of enquiring, on what do you chiefly subsist?"

"Mainly on oyster patties," said the Bluebottle Fly; "and, when these are scarce, on raspberry vinegar and Russian leather boiled down to a jelly."

"How delicious!" said Guy.

To which Lionel added, "Huzz!" And all the Bluebottle Flies said, "Buzz!"

At this time, an elderly Fly said it was the hour for the evening song to be sung; and, on a signal being given, all the Bluebottle Flies began to buzz at once in a sumptuous and sonorous manner, the melodious and mucilaginous sounds echoing all over the waters and resounding across the tumultuous tops of the transitory titmice upon the intervening and verdant mountains with a serene and sickly suavity only known to the truly virtuous. The moon was shining slobaciously from the star-bespangled sky, while her light irrigated the smooth and shiny sides and wings and backs of the Bluebottle Flies with a peculiar and trivial splendour, while all Nature cheerfully responded to the cerulean and conspicuous circumstances.

In many long-after years, the four little travellers looked back to that evening as one of the happiest in all their lives; and it was already past midnight when – the sail of the boat having been set up by the Quangle-Wangle, the tea kettle and churn placed in their respective positions, and the Pussy Cat stationed at the helm – the children each took a last and affectionate farewell of the Bluebottle Flies, who walked down in a body to the water's edge to see the travellers embark.

As a token of parting respect and esteem, Violet made a curtsy quite down to the ground, and stuck one of her few remaining parrot-tail feathers into the back hair of the most pleasing of the Bluebottle Flies, while Slingsby, Guy and Lionel offered them three small boxes, containing, respectively, black pins, dried figs and Epsom salts – and thus they left that happy shore for ever.

Overcome by their feelings, the four little travellers instantly jumped into the tea kettle and fell fast asleep. But all along the shore, for many hours, there was distinctly heard a sound of severely suppressed sobs, and of a vague multitude of living creatures using their pocket handkerchiefs in a subdued simultaneous snuffle, lingering sadly along the walloping waves as the boat sailed further and further away from the Land of the Happy Bluebottle Flies.

Nothing particular occurred for some days after these events, except that, as the travellers were passing a low tract of sand, they perceived an unusual and gratifying spectacle: namely, a large number of Crabs and Crawfish – perhaps six or seven hundred – sitting by the waterside and endeavouring to disentangle a vast heap of pale pink worsted, which they moistened at intervals with a fluid composed of lavender water and white-wine negus.

"Can we be of any service to you, O crusty Crabbies?" said the four children.

"Thank you kindly," said the Crabs consecutively. "We are trying to make some worsted mittens, but do not know how."

On which Violet, who was perfectly acquainted with the art of mitten-making, said to the Crabs, "Do your claws unscrew, or are they fixtures?"

"They are all made to unscrew," said the Crabs; and forthwith they deposited a great pile of claws close to the boat, with which Violet uncombed all the pale pink worsted, and then made the loveliest mittens with it you can imagine. These the Crabs, having resumed and screwed on their claws, placed cheerfully upon their wrists, and walked away rapidly on their hind legs, warbling songs with a silvery voice and in a minor key.

After this, the four little people sailed on again till they came to a vast and wide plain of astonishing dimensions, on which nothing whatever could be discovered at first; but, as the travellers walked onward, there appeared in the extreme and dim distance a single object, which on a nearer approach, and on an accurately cutaneous inspection, seemed to be somebody in a large white wig sitting on an armchair made of sponge cakes and oyster shells. "It does not quite look like a human being," said Violet doubtfully; nor could they make out what it really was till the Quangle-Wangle (who had previously been round the world) exclaimed softly in a loud voice "It is the cooperative Cauliflower!"

And so, in truth, it was – and they soon found that what they had taken for an immense wig was in reality the top of the Cauliflower; and that he had no feet at all, being able to walk tolerably well with a fluctuating and graceful movement on a single cabbage stalk – an accomplishment which naturally saved him the expense of stockings and shoes.

Presently, while the whole party from the boat was gazing at him with mingled affection and disgust, he suddenly arose, and, in a somewhat plumdomphious manner, hurried off towards the setting sun – his steps supported by two superincumbent confidential Cucumbers, and a large number of Waterwagtails proceeding in advance of him by three and three in a row – till he finally disappeared on the brink of the western sky in a crystal cloud of sudorific sand.

So remarkable a sight, of course, impressed the four children very deeply; and they returned immediately to their boat with a strong sense of undeveloped asthma and a great appetite.

Shortly after this, the travellers were obliged to sail directly below some high overhanging rocks, from the top of one of which a particularly odious little boy, dressed in rose-coloured knickerbockers, and with a pewter

plate upon his head, threw an enormous pumpkin at the boat, by which
it was instantly upset.

But this upsetting was of no consequence, because all the party knew how
to swim very well – and, in fact, they preferred swimming about till after
the moon rose; when, the water growing chilly, they sponge-taneously
entered the boat. Meanwhile, the Quangle-Wangle threw back the pumpkin with immense force, so that it hit the rocks where the malicious little
boy in rose-coloured knickerbockers was sitting; when, being quite full
of lucifer matches, the pumpkin exploded surreptitiously into a thousand
bits; whereon the rocks instantly took fire, and the odious little boy became
unpleasantly hotter and hotter and hotter, till his knickerbockers were
turned quite green and his nose was burnt off.

Two or three days after this had happened, they came to another place,
where they found nothing at all except some wide and deep pits full of
mulberry jam. This is the property of the tiny, yellow-nosed Apes who
abound in these districts, and who store up the mulberry jam for their food
in winter, when they mix it with pellucid pale periwinkle soup and serve
it out in Wedgwood china bowls, which grow freely all over that part of
the country. Only one of the yellow-nosed Apes was on the spot, and he
was fast asleep; yet the four travellers and the Quangle-Wangle and Pussy
were so terrified by the violence and sanguinary sound of his snoring that
they merely took a small cupful of the jam and returned to re-embark in
their boat without delay.

What was their horror on seeing the boat (including the churn and
the tea kettle) in the mouth of an enormous Seeze Pyder, an aquatic and
ferocious creature truly dreadful to behold, and, happily, only met with
in those excessive longitudes! In a moment, the beautiful boat was bitten
into fifty-five thousand million hundred billion bits; and it instantly
became quite clear that Violet, Slingsby, Guy and Lionel could no longer
preliminate their voyage by sea.

The four travellers were therefore obliged to resolve on pursuing their wanderings by land – and, very fortunately, there happened to pass by at that moment an elderly Rhinoceros, on which they seized; and, all four mounting on his back – the Quangle-Wangle sitting on his horn and holding on by his ears, and the Pussy Cat swinging at the end of his tail – they set off, having only four small beans and three pounds of mashed potatoes to last through their whole journey.

They were, however, able to catch numbers of the chickens and turkeys and other birds who incessantly alighted on the head of the Rhinoceros for the purpose of gathering the seeds of the rhododendron plants which grew there; and these creatures they cooked in the most translucent and satisfactory manner by means of a fire lighted on the end of the Rhinoceros's back. A crowd of Kangaroos and gigantic Cranes accompanied them, from feelings of curiosity and complacency; so that they were never at a loss for company, and went onward, as it were, in a sort of profuse and triumphant procession.

Thus in less than eighteen weeks they all arrived safely at home, where they were received by their admiring relatives with joy tempered with contempt, and where they finally resolved to carry out the rest of their travelling plans at some more favourable opportunity.

As for the Rhinoceros, in token of their grateful adherence, they had him killed and stuffed directly, and then set him up outside the door of their father's house as a diaphanous doorscraper.

THE HISTORY OF
THE SEVEN FAMILIES
OF THE LAKE PIPPLE-POPPLE

CHAPTER I

INTRODUCTORY

In former days – that is to say, once upon a time – there lived, in the Land of Gramble-Blamble, seven families. They lived by the side of the great Lake Pipple-Popple (one of the seven families, indeed, lived *in* the lake), and on the outskirts of the city of Tosh – which, excepting when it was quite dark, they could see plainly. The names of all these places you have probably heard of – and you have only not to look in your geography books to find out all about them.

Now, the seven families who lived on the borders of the great Lake Pipple-Popple were as follows in the next chapter.

CHAPTER II

THE SEVEN FAMILIES

There was a family of two old Parrots and seven young Parrots.

There was a family of two old Storks and seven young Storks.

There was a family of two old Geese and seven young Geese.

There was a family of two old Owls and seven young Owls.

There was a family of two old Guinea Pigs and seven young Guinea Pigs.

There was a family of two old Cats and seven young Cats.

And there was a family of two old Fishes and seven young Fishes.

CHAPTER III

THE HABITS OF THE SEVEN FAMILIES

The Parrots lived upon the soffsky-poffsky trees, which were beautiful to behold and covered with blue leaves, and they fed upon fruit, artichokes and striped beetles.

The Storks walked in and out of the Lake Pipple-Popple, and ate frogs for breakfast and buttered toast for tea; but on account of the extreme length of their legs, they could not sit down, and so they walked about continually.

The Geese, having webs to their feet, caught quantities of flies, which they ate for dinner.

The Owls anxiously looked after mice, which they caught and made into sago puddings.

The Guinea Pigs toddled about the gardens and ate lettuces and Cheshire cheese.

The Cats sat still in the sunshine and fed upon sponge biscuits.

The Fishes lived in the lake and fed chiefly on boiled periwinkles.

And all these seven families lived together in the utmost fun and felicity.

CHAPTER IV

THE CHILDREN OF THE SEVEN FAMILIES ARE SENT AWAY

One day, all the seven fathers and the seven mothers of the seven families agreed that they would send their children out to see the world.

So they called them all together and gave them each eight shillings and some good advice, some chocolate drops and a small green morocco pocket-book to set down their expenses in.

They then particularly entreated them not to quarrel – and all the parents sent off their children with a parting injunction.

"If," said the old Parrots, "you find a cherry, do not fight about who should have it."

"And," said the old Storks, "if you find a frog, divide it carefully into seven bits, but on no account quarrel about it."

And the old Geese said to the seven young Geese, "Whatever you do, be sure you do not touch a plum-pudding flea."

And the old Owls said, "If you find a mouse, tear him up into seven slices and eat him cheerfully, but without quarrelling."

And the old Guinea Pigs said, "Have a care that you eat your lettuces, should you find any, not greedily, but calmly."

And the old Cats said, "Be particularly careful not to meddle with a clangle-wangle, if you should see one."

And the old Fishes said, "Above all things, avoid eating a blue boss-woss, for they do not agree with fishes, and give them a pain in their toes."

So all the children of each family thanked their parents – and, making in all forty-nine polite bows, they went into the wide world.

CHAPTER V

THE HISTORY OF THE SEVEN YOUNG PARROTS

The seven young Parrots had not gone far when they saw a tree with a single cherry on it, which the oldest Parrot picked instantly; but the other six, being extremely hungry, tried to get it also. On which all the seven began to fight – and they scuffled,

and huffled,

and ruffled,

and shuffled,

and puffled,

and muffled,

and buffled,

and duffled,

and fluffled,

and guffled,

and bruffled, and

screamed, and shrieked, and squealed,

and squeaked, and clawed, and snapped, and bit, and bumped, and thumped, and dumped, and flumped each other, till they were all torn into little bits; and at last there was nothing left to record this painful incident except the cherry and seven small green feathers.

And that was the vicious and voluble end of the seven young Parrots.

CHAPTER VI

THE HISTORY OF THE SEVEN YOUNG STORKS

When the seven young Storks set out, they walked or flew for fourteen weeks in a straight line, and for six weeks more in a crooked one; and after that they ran as hard as they could for one hundred and eight miles; and after that they stood still, and made a himmeltanious chatter-clatter-blattery noise with their bills.

About the same time, they perceived a large frog, spotted with green and with a sky-blue stripe under each ear.

So, being hungry, they immediately flew at him, and were going to divide him into seven pieces when they began to quarrel as to which of his legs should be taken off first. One said this, and another said that; and while they were all quarrelling, the frog hopped away. And when they saw that he was gone, they began to chatter-clatter

blatter-platter,
patter-blatter,
matter-clatter,

flatter-quatter more violently than ever; and after they had fought for a week, they pecked each other all to little pieces, so that at last nothing was left of any of them except their bills.

And that was the end of the seven young Storks.

CHAPTER VII

When the seven young Geese began to travel, they went over a large plain, on which there was but one tree, and that was a very bad one.

So four of them went up to the top of it and looked about them, while the other three waddled up and down and repeated poetry, and their last six lessons in arithmetic, geography and cookery.

Presently they perceived, a long way off, an object of the most interesting and obese appearance, having a perfectly round body exactly resembling a boiled plum pudding, with two little wings and a beak, and three feathers growing out of his head, and only one leg.

So, after a time, all the seven young Geese said to each other, "Beyond all doubt, this beast must be a Plum-Pudding Flea!"

On which they incautiously began to sing aloud,

> Plum-Pudding Flea,
> Plum-Pudding Flea,
> Wherever you be,
> Oh, come to our tree
> And listen, oh, listen, oh, listen to me!

And no sooner had they sung this verse than the Plum-Pudding Flea began to hop and skip on his one leg with the most dreadful velocity, and came straight to the tree, where he stopped and looked about him in a vacant and voluminous manner.

On which the seven young Geese were greatly alarmed, and all of a tremble-bemble – so one of them put out his long neck and just touched him with the tip of his bill; but no sooner had he done this than the Plum-Pudding Flea skipped and hopped about more and more and higher and higher; after which, he opened his mouth and, to the great surprise and indignation of the seven Geese, began to bark so loudly and furiously and terribly that they were totally unable to bear the noise; and by degrees every one of them suddenly tumbled down quite dead.

So that was the end of the seven young Geese.

CHAPTER VIII

THE HISTORY OF THE SEVEN YOUNG OWLS

When the seven young Owls set out, they sat every now and then on the branches of old trees, and never went far at one time.

And one night, when it was quite dark, they thought they heard a mouse; but, as the gas lamps were not lighted, they could not see him.

So they called out, "Is that a mouse?"

On which a mouse answered, "Squeaky-peeky-weeky! Yes, it is!"

And immediately all the young Owls threw themselves off the tree, meaning to alight on the ground; but they did not perceive that there was a large well below them, into which they all fell superficially, and were every one of them drowned in less than half a minute.

So that was the end of the seven young Owls.

CHAPTER IX

THE HISTORY OF THE SEVEN YOUNG GUINEA PIGS

The seven young Guinea Pigs went into a garden full of gooseberry bushes and tiggory trees, under one of which they fell asleep. When they awoke, they saw a large lettuce, which had grown out of the ground while they had been sleeping, and which had an immense number of green leaves. At which they all exclaimed,

> Lettuce, O lettuce,
> Let us, oh let us,
> O lettuce leaves,
> Oh let us leave this tree and eat
> Lettuce, oh let us, lettuce leaves!

An instantly the seven young Guinea Pigs rushed with such extreme force against the lettuce plant, and hit their heads so vividly against its stalk, that the concussion brought on directly an incipient transitional inflammation of their noses, which grew worse and worse and worse and worse, till it incidentally killed them all seven.

And that was the end of the seven young Guinea Pigs.

CHAPTER X

THE HISTORY OF THE SEVEN YOUNG CATS

The seven young Cats set off on their travels with great delight and rapacity. But, on coming to the top of a high hill, they perceived at a long distance off a clangle-wangle (or, as it is more properly written, clangel-wangel); and, in spite of the warning they had had, they ran straight up to it.

(Now, the Clangle-Wangle is a most dangerous and delusive beast, and by no means commonly to be met with. They live in the water as well as on land, using their long tail as a sail when in the former element. Their speed is extreme; but their habits of life are domestic and superfluous, and their general demeanour pensive and pellucid. On summer evenings, they may sometimes be observed near the Lake Pipple-Popple, standing on their heads and humming their national melodies. They subsist entirely on vegetables, excepting when they eat veal or mutton or pork or beef or fish or saltpetre.)

The moment the Clangle-Wangle saw the seven young Cats approach, he ran away – and as he ran straight on for four months, and the Cats, though they continued to run, could never overtake him, they all gradually *died* of fatigue and exhaustion, and never afterwards recovered.

And this was the end of the seven young Cats.

CHAPTER XI

THE HISTORY OF THE SEVEN FISHES

The seven young Fishes swam across the Lake Pipple-Popple, and into the river, and into the ocean – where, most unhappily for them, they saw, on the fifteenth day of their travels, a bright-blue boss-woss, and instantly swam after him. But the blue Boss-Woss plunged into a perpendicular,
           spicular,
          orbicular
           quadrangular,
            circular depth of soft mud –
where, in fact, his house was.

And the seven young Fishes, swimming with great and uncomfortable velocity, plunged also into the mud quite against their will, and, not being accustomed to it, were all suffocated in a very short period.

And that was the end of the seven young Fishes.

CHAPTER XII

OF WHAT OCCURRED SUBSEQUENTLY

After it was known that the

           seven young Parrots,
     and the seven young Storks,
     and the seven young Geese,
     and the seven young Owls,
     and the seven young Guinea Pigs,
     and the seven young Cats,
     and the seven young Fishes

were all dead, then the Frog, and the Plum-Pudding Flea, and the Mouse, and the Clangle-Wangle, and the blue Boss-Woss, all met together to rejoice over their good fortune. And they collected the seven feathers of the seven young Parrots, and the seven bills of the seven young Storks, and the lettuce, and the cherry; and having placed the latter on the lettuce, and the other objects in a circular arrangement at their base, they danced a hornpipe round all these memorials until they were quite tired; after which, they gave a tea party, and a garden party, and a ball, and a concert, and then returned to their respective homes full of joy and respect, sympathy, satisfaction and disgust.

CHAPTER XIII

OF WHAT BECAME OF THE PARENTS
OF THE FORTY-NINE CHILDREN

But when the two old Parrots,

> and the two old Storks,
> and the two old Geese,
> and the two old Owls,
> and the two old Guinea Pigs,
> and the two old Cats,
> and the two old Fishes

became aware, by reading in the newspapers, of the calamitous extinction of the whole of their families, they refused all further sustenance; and, sending out to various shops, they purchased great quantities of cayenne pepper and brandy and vinegar and blue sealing wax, besides seven immense glass bottles with airtight stoppers. And, having done this, they ate a light supper of brown bread and Jerusalem artichokes, and took an affecting and formal leave of the whole of their acquaintance, which was very numerous and distinguished and select and responsible and ridiculous.

CHAPTER XIV

CONCLUSION

And after this they filled the bottles with the ingredients for pickling, and each couple jumped into a separate bottle; by which effort, of course, they all died immediately, and became thoroughly pickled in a few minutes having previously made their wills (by the assistance of the most eminent lawyers of the district), in which they left strict orders that the stopper of the seven bottles should be carefully sealed up with the blue sealing wax they had purchased; and that they themselves, in the bottles, should be presented to the principal museum of the city of Tosh, to be labelled with parchment or any other anti-congenial succedaneum, and to be placed on a marble table with silver-gilt legs for the daily inspection and contemplation, and for the perpetual benefit, of the pusillanimous public.

And if you ever happen to go to Gramble-Blamble and visit that museum in the city of Tosh, look for them on the ninety-eighth table in the four hundred and twenty-seventh room of the right-hand corridor of the left wing of the central quadrangle of that magnificent building – for, if you do not, you certainly will not see them.

MORE NONSENSE

INTRODUCTION

In offering this little book – the third of its kind – to the public, I am glad to take the opportunity of recording the pleasure I have received at the appreciation its predecessors have met with, as attested by their wide circulation and by the universally kind notices of them from the press. To have been the means of administering innocent mirth to thousands may surely be a just motive for satisfaction, and an excuse for grateful expression.

At the same time, I am desirous of adding a few words as to the history of the two previously published volumes, and more particularly of the first or original *Book of Nonsense*, relating to which many absurd reports have crept into circulation, such as that it was the composition of the late Lord Brougham, the late Earl of Derby, etc. – that the rhymes and pictures are by different persons, or that the whole have a symbolical meaning, etc., etc. – whereas every one of the rhymes was composed by myself, and every one of the illustrations drawn by my own hand at the time the verses were made. Moreover, in no portion of these nonsense drawings have I ever allowed any caricature of private or public persons to appear, and throughout, more care than might be supposed has been given to make the subjects incapable of misinterpretation – "nonsense", pure and absolute, having been my aim throughout.

As for the persistently absurd report of the late Earl of Derby being the author of the first *Book of Nonsense*, I may relate an incident which occurred to me four summers ago, the first that gave me any insight into the origin of the rumour.

I was on my way from London to Guildford, in a railway carriage containing, besides myself, one passenger, an elderly gentleman. Presently, however, two ladies entered, accompanied by two little boys. These, who had just had a copy of the *Book of Nonsense* given them, were loud in their delight, and by degrees infected the whole party with their mirth.

"How grateful," said the old gentleman to the two ladies, "all children and parents too ought to be to the statesman who has given his time to composing that charming book!"

(The ladies looked puzzled, as indeed was I, the author.)

"Do you not know who is the writer of it?" asked the gentleman.

"The name is 'Edward Lear'," said one of the ladies.

"Ah!" said the first speaker. "So it is printed – but that is only a whim of the real author, the Earl of Derby. 'Edward' is his Christian name – and, as you may see, LEAR is only EARL transposed."

"But," said the lady doubtingly, "here is a dedication to the great-grandchildren, grand-nephews and grand-nieces of Edward, thirteenth Earl of Derby, by the author, Edward Lear."

"That," replied the other, "is simply a piece of mystification; I am in a position to know that the whole book was composed and illustrated by Lord Derby himself. In fact, there is no such a person at all as Edward Lear."

"Yet," said the other lady, "some friends of mine tell me they know Mr Lear."

"Quite a mistake! Completely a mistake!" said the old gentleman, becoming rather angry at the contradiction. "I am well aware of what I am saying. I can inform you, no such a person as 'Edward Lear' exists!"

Hitherto I had kept silence, but as my hat was – as well as my handkerchief and stick – largely marked inside with my name, and as I happened to have in my pocket several letters addressed to me, the temptation was too great to resist: so, flashing all these articles at once on my would-be extinguisher's attention, I speedily reduced him to silence.

The second volume of "nonsense", commencing with the verses 'The Owl and the Pussy Cat', was written at different times and for different sets of children; the whole being collected in the course of last year, were then illustrated and published in a single volume by Mr R.J. Bush of 32 Charing Cross.

The contents of the third or present volume were made also at different intervals in the last two years.

Long years ago, in days when much of my time was passed in a country house where children and mirth abounded, the lines beginning "There was an old man of Tobago" were suggested to me by a valued friend as a form of verse lending itself to limitless variety for rhymes and pictures – and thenceforth the greater part of the original drawings and verses for the first *Book of Nonsense* were struck off with a pen, no assistance ever having been given me in any way but that of uproarious delight and welcome at the appearance of every new absurdity.

Most of these drawings and rhymes were transferred to lithographic stones in the year 1846 and were then first published by Mr Thomas McLean of the Haymarket. But that edition having been soon exhausted, and the call for the *Book of Nonsense* continuing, I added a considerable number of subjects to those previously published, and having caused the whole to be carefully reproduced in woodcuts by Messrs Dalzell, I disposed of the copyright to Messrs Routledge and Warne, by whom the volume was published in 1861.

EDWARD LEAR

Villa Emily, Sanremo,
    August 1871

ONE HUNDRED NONSENSE
PICTURES AND RHYMES

1.   There was a young person of Bantry
         Who frequently slept in the pantry;
            When disturbed by the mice,
            She appeased them with rice,
         That judicious young person of Bantry.

2.　　There was an old man at a junction
　　　Whose feelings were wrung with compunction;
　　　　　When they said, "The Train's gone!"
　　　　　He exclaimed, "How forlorn!"
　　　But remained on the rails of the junction.

3.　　There was an old man who, when little,
　　　Fell casually into a kettle;
　　　　　But, growing too stout,
　　　　　He could never get out,
　　　So he passed all his life in that kettle.

4. There was an old man whose despair
   Induced him to purchase a hare;
     Whereon one fine day
     He rode wholly away,
   Which partly assuaged his despair.

5. There was an old person of Minety
   Who purchased five hundred and ninety
     Large apples and pears,
     Which he threw unawares
   At the heads of the people of Minety.

6. There was an old man of Thermopylae
   Who never did anything properly;
   But they said, "If you choose
   To boil eggs in your shoes,
   You shall never remain in Thermopylae."

7. There was an old person of Deal
   Who in walking used only his heel;
   When they said, "Tell us why"
   He made no reply,
   That mysterious old person of Deal.

8.   There was an old man on the Humber
        Who dined on a cake of burnt umber;
           When he said, "It's enough!"
           They only said, "Stuff!
        You amazing old man on the Humber!"

9.   There was an old man of Blackheath
        Whose head was adorned with a wreath
           Of lobsters and spice,
           Pickled onions and mice,
        That uncommon old man of Blackheath.

10.   There was an old man of Toulouse
       Who purchased a new pair of shoes;
          When they asked, "Are they pleasant?"
          He said, "Not at present!"
       That turbid old man of Toulouse.

11.   There was an old person in black –
       A grasshopper jumped on his back;
          When it chirped in his ear,
          He was smitten with fear,
       That helpless old person in black.

12. There was an old man in a barge
   Whose nose was exceedingly large;
     But, in fishing by night,
     It supported a light,
   Which helped that old man in a barge.

13. There was an old man of Dunrose –
   A parrot seized hold of his nose.
     When he grew melancholy,
     They said, "His name's Polly" –
   Which soothed that old man of Dunrose.

14.   There was an old person of Bromley
      Whose ways were not cheerful or comely;
         He sat in the dust
         Eating spiders and crust,
      That unpleasing old person of Bromley.

15.   There was an old man of Dunluce
      Who went out to sea on a goose;
         When he'd gone out a mile,
         He observed with a smile,
      "It is time to return to Dunluce."

16.   There was an old person of Pinner
         As thin as a lath, if not thinner;
            They dressed him in white
            And rolled him up tight,
         That elastic old person of Pinner.

17.   There was an old man in a marsh
         Whose manners were futile and harsh;
            He sat on a log
            And sang songs to a frog,
         That instructive old man in a marsh.

18.   There was an old man of Deeside
        Whose hat was exceedingly wide;
           But he said, "Do not fail,
           If it happen to hail,
        To come under my hat at Deeside!"

19.   There was an old person of Bree,
        Who frequented the depths of the sea;
           She nursed the small fishes
           And washed all the dishes,
        And swam back again into Bree.

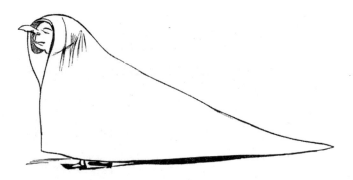

20.   There was a young person in green
Who seldom was fit to be seen;
    She wore a long shawl
    Over bonnet and all,
Which enveloped that person in green.

21.   There was an old person of Wick
Who said, "Tick-a-Tick, Tick-a-Tick;
    Chickabee, Chickabaw."
    And he said nothing more,
That laconic old person of Wick.

22.   There was an old man at a station
       Who made a promiscuous oration;
          But they said, "Take some snuff!
          You have talked quite enough,
       You afflicting old man at a station!"

23.   There was an old man of Three Bridges
       Whose mind was distracted by midges;
          He sat on a wheel
          Eating underdone veal,
       Which relieved that old man of Three Bridges.

24.   There was an old person of Fife
        Who was greatly disgusted with life;
           They sang him a ballad
           And fed him on salad,
        Which cured that old person of Fife.

25.   There was an old person of Shields
        Who frequented the valleys and fields;
           All the mice and the cats,
           And the snakes and the rats,
        Followed after that person of Shields.

26.   There was an old person of China
       Whose daughters were Jiska and Dinah,
          Amelia and Fluffy,
          Olivia and Chuffy,
       And all of them settled in China.

27.   There was an old man of the Dargle
       Who purchased six barrels of gargle;
          For he said, "I'll sit still,
          And will roll them downhill,
       For the fish in the depths of the Dargle."

28. There was an old man who screamed out
    Whenever they knocked him about;
       So they took off his boots
       And fed him with fruits,
    And continued to knock him about.

29. There was an old person of Brill
    Who purchased a shirt with a frill;
       But they said, "Don't you wish
       You mayn't look like a fish,
    You obsequious old person of Brill?"

30.   There was an old person of Slough
       Who danced at the end of a bough;
           But they said, "If you sneeze,
           You might damage the trees,
       You imprudent old person of Slough."

31.   There was a young person in red
       Who carefully covered her head
           With a bonnet of leather
           And three lines of feather,
       Besides some long ribbons of red.

32.   There was a young person in pink
Who called out for something to drink;
    But they said, "Oh, my daughter,
    There's nothing but water!" –
Which vexed that young person in pink.

33.   There was a young lady in white
Who looked out at the depths of the night;
    But the birds of the air
    Filled her heart with despair
And oppressed that young lady in white.

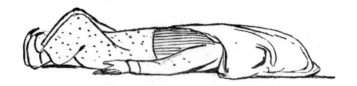

34.   There was an old man of Hong Kong
Who never did anything wrong;
    He lay on his back
    With his head in a sack,
That innocuous old man of Hong Kong.

35.   There was an old person of Putney
Whose food was roast spiders and chutney,
    Which he took with his tea
    Within sight of the sea,
That romantic old person of Putney.

36.   There was an old person of Woking
       Whose mind was perverse and provoking;
            He sat on a rail
            With his head in a pail,
       That illusive old person of Woking.

37.   There was an old lady of France
       Who taught little ducklings to dance;
            When she said, "Tick-a-tack!"
            They only said, "Quack!" –
       Which grieved that old lady of France.

38.   There was a young lady in blue
        Who said, "Is it you? Is it you?"
            When they said, "Yes, it is"
            She replied only, "Whizz!" –
    That ungracious young lady in blue.

39.   There was an old man in a garden
        Who always begged everyone's pardon;
            When they asked him, "What for?"
            He replied, "You're a bore!
    And I trust you'll go out of my garden."

40. There was an old person of Loo
Who said, "What on earth shall I do?"
    When they said, "Go away!"
    She continued to stay,
That vexatious old person of Loo.

41. There was an old person of Pisa
Whose daughters did nothing to please her;
    She dressed them in grey
    And banged them all day
Round the walls of the city of Pisa.

42.   There was an old person of Florence
       Who held mutton chops in abhorrence;
          He purchased a bustard
          And fried him in mustard,
       Which choked that old person of Florence.

43.   There was an old person of Sheen
       Whose expression was calm and serene;
          He sat in the water
          And drank bottled porter,
      That placid old person of Sheen.

44. There was an old person of Ware
     Who rode on the back of a bear;
         When they asked, "Does it trot?"
         He said, "Certainly not!
     He's a Moppsikon Floppsikon bear!"

45. There was an old person of Dean
     Who dined on one pea and one bean;
         For he said, "More than that
         Would make me too fat" –
     That cautious old person of Dean.

46.   There was a young person of Janina
      Whose uncle was always a-fanning her;
        When he fanned off her head,
        She smiled sweetly and said,
    "You propitious old person of Janina!"

47.   There was an old person of Down
      Whose face was adorned with a frown;
        When he opened the door
        For one minute or more,
    He alarmed all the people of Down.

48. There was an old person of Cassel
    Whose nose finished off in a tassel;
     But they called out, "Oh well!
     Don't it look like a bell!" –
    Which perplexed that old person of Cassel.

49. There was an old man of Kashmir
    Whose movements were scroobious and queer;
     Being slender and tall,
     He looked over a wall
    And perceived two fat ducks of Kashmir.

50.   There was an old person of Hove
       Who frequented the depths of a grove,
            Where he studied his books
            With the wrens and the rooks,
       That tranquil old person of Hove.

51.   There was an old man of Spithead
       Who opened the window and said,
            "Fil-jomble, fil-jumble,
            Fil-rumble-come-tumble!" –
       That doubtful old man of Spithead.

52.   There was an old man on the border
        Who lived in the utmost disorder;
            He danced with the cat
            And made tea in his hat –
        Which vexed all the folks on the border.

53.   There was an old man of Dundalk
        Who tried to teach fishes to walk;
            When they tumbled down dead,
            He grew weary and said,
        "I had better go back to Dundalk!"

54. There was an old man of Dumbree
Who taught little owls to drink tea;
   For he said, "To eat mice
   Is not proper or nice" –
That amiable man of Dumbree.

55. There was an old person of Jodd
Whose ways were perplexing and odd;
   She purchased a whistle
   And sat on a thistle,
And squeaked to the people of Jodd.

56. There was an old person of Shoreham
     Whose habits were marked by decorum;
         He bought an umbrella
         And sat in the cellar –
     Which pleased all the people of Shoreham.

57. There was an old man whose remorse
     Induced him to drink caper sauce;
         For they said, "If mixed up
         With some cold claret cup,
     It will certainly soothe your remorse!"

58. There was an old person of Wilts
    Who constantly walked upon stilts;
        He wreathed them with lilies
        And daffydowndillies,
    That elegant person of Wilts.

59. There was an old person of Newry
    Whose manners were tinctured with fury;
        He tore all the rugs
        And broke all the jugs
    Within twenty miles' distance of Newry.

60.   There was an old person of Pett
        Who was partly consumed by regret;
            He sat in a cart
            And ate cold apple tart,
        Which relieved that old person of Pett.

61.   There was an old man of Port Grigor
        Whose actions were noted for vigour;
            He stood on his head
            Till his waistcoat turned red,
        That eclectic old man of Port Grigor.

62.   There was an old person of Barr
        Who passed all her life in a jar,
            Which she painted pea-green
            To appear more serene,
        That placid old person of Barr.

63.   There was an old man of West Dumpet
        Who possessed a large nose like a trumpet;
            When he blew it aloud,
            It astonished the crowd,
        And was heard through the whole of West Dumpet.

64.   There was an old person of Grange
        Whose manners were scroobious and strange;
           He sailed to St Blubb
           In a waterproof tub,
        That aquatic old person of Grange.

65.   There was an old person of Nice
        Whose associates were usually geese;
           They walked out together
           In all sorts of weather –
        That affable person of Nice!

66.   There was a young person of Kew
       Whose virtues and vices were few;
          But with blamable haste
          She devoured some hot paste,
       Which destroyed that young person of Kew.

67.   There was an old person of Sark
       Who made an unpleasant remark;
          But they said, "Don't you see
          What a brute you must be,
       You obnoxious old person of Sark?"

68.   There was an old person of Filey,
Of whom his acquaintance spoke highly;
   He danced perfectly well
   To the sound of a bell,
And delighted the people of Filey.

69.   There was an old man of El Hums
Who lived upon nothing but crumbs,
   Which he picked off the ground,
   With the other birds round,
In the roads and the lanes of El Hums.

70.   There was an old man of Dunblane
       Who greatly resembled a crane;
          But they said, "Is it wrong,
          Since your legs are so long,
       To request you won't stay in Dunblane?"

71.   There was an old person of Hyde
       Who walked by the shore with his bride,
          Till a crab who came near
          Filled their bosoms with fear,
      And they said, "Would we'd never left Hyde!"

72.   There was an old person of Rimini
        Who said, "Gracious! Goodness! Oh, Jimini!"
            When they said, "Please be still!"
            She ran down a hill,
      And was never more heard of at Rimini.

73.   There was an old person of Cannes
        Who purchased three fowls and a fan;
            Those she placed on a stool,
            And, to make them feel cool,
      She constantly fanned them at Cannes.

74.　　There was an old person of Bude
　　　　Whose deportment was vicious and crude;
　　　　　　He wore a large ruff
　　　　　　Of pale straw-coloured stuff,
　　　　Which perplexed all the people of Bude.

75.　　There was an old person of Ickley
　　　　Who could not abide to ride quickly;
　　　　　　He rode to Karnak
　　　　　　On a tortoise's back,
　　　　That moony old person of Ickley.

76.　There was an old man of Ancona
　　　Who found a small dog with no owner,
　　　　　Which he took up and down
　　　　　All the streets of the town –
　　　That anxious old man of Ancona.

77.　There was an old person of Barnes
　　　Whose garments were covered with darns;
　　　　　But they said, "Without doubt,
　　　　　You will soon wear them out,
　　　You luminous person of Barnes!"

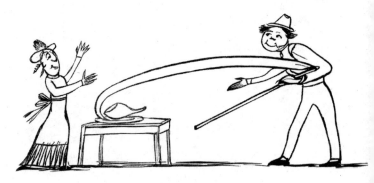

78.   There was an old person of Blythe
Who cut up his meat with a scythe;
    When they said, "Well, I never!"
    He cried, "Scythes for ever!" –
That lively old person of Blythe.

79.   There was an old person of Ealing
Who was wholly devoid of good feeling;
    He drove a small gig,
    With three owls and a pig,
Which distressed all the people of Ealing.

80.   There was an old person of Bray
Who sang through the whole of the day
To his ducks and his pigs,
Whom he fed upon figs,
That valuable person of Bray.

81.   There was an old person of Bow
Whom nobody happened to know;
So they gave him some soap
And said coldly, "We hope
You will go back directly to Bow!"

82.   There was an old person in grey
Whose feelings were tinged with dismay;
    She purchased two parrots
    And fed them with carrots,
Which pleased that old person in grey.

83.   There was an old person of Crowle
Who lived in the nest of an owl;
    When they screamed in the nest,
    He screamed out with the rest,
That depressing old person of Crowle.

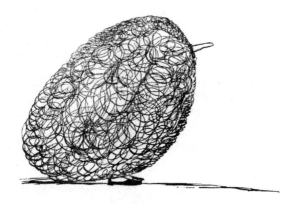

84.   There was an old person of Brigg
        Who purchased no end of a wig;
           So that only his nose
           And the end of his toes
        Could be seen when he walked about Brigg.

85.   There was a young lady of Greenwich
        Whose garments were bordered with spinach;
           But a large spotty calf
           Bit her shawl quite in half,
        Which alarmed that young lady of Greenwich.

86.   There was an old person of Rye
      Who went up to town on a fly;
         But they said, "If you cough,
         You are safe to fall off,
      You abstemious old person of Rye!"

87.   There was an old man of Messina
      Whose daughter was named Opsibeena;
         She wore a small wig
         And rode out on a pig,
      To the perfect delight of Messina.

88.   There is a young lady whose nose
Continually prospers and grows;
   When it grew out of sight,
   She exclaimed in a fright,
"Oh, farewell to the end of my nose!"

89.   There was an old person of Sestri
Who sat himself down in the vestry;
   When they said, "You are wrong!"
   He merely said, "Bong!" –
That repulsive old person of Sestri.

90.   There was an old man in a tree
Whose whiskers were lovely to see;
    But the birds of the air
    Plucked them perfectly bare,
To make themselves nests in that tree.

91.   There was a young lady of Corsica
Who purchased a little brown saucy cur,
    Which she fed upon ham
    And hot raspberry jam,
That expensive young lady of Corsica.

92.   There was a young lady of Firle
      Whose hair was addicted to curl;
          It curled up a tree
          And all over the sea,
      That expansive young lady of Firle.

93.   There was an old lady of Winchelsea
      Who said, "If you needle or pin shall see
          On the floor of my room,
          Sweep it up with the broom!" –
      That exhaustive old Lady of Winchelsea!

94.   There was a young person whose history
       Was always considered a mystery;
          She sat in a ditch,
          Although no one knew which,
       And composed a small treatise on history.

95.   There was an old man of Boulak
       Who sat on a crocodile's back;
          But they said, "Tow'rds the night
          He may probably bite,
       Which might vex you, old man of Boulak!"

96.   There was an old man of Ibreem
       Who suddenly threatened to scream;
          But they said, "If you do,
          We will thump you quite blue,
       You disgusting old man of Ibreem!"

97.   There was an old person of Stroud
       Who was horribly jammed in a crowd;
          Some she slew with a kick,
          Some she scrunched with a stick,
       That impulsive old person of Stroud.

98.   There was an old man of Thames Ditton
        Who called out for something to sit on;
            But they brought him a hat
            And said, "Sit upon that,
        You abruptious old man of Thames Ditton!"

99.   There was an old person of Skye
        Who waltzed with a bluebottle fly;
            They buzzed a sweet tune
            To the light of the moon
        And entranced all the people of Skye.

100. There was a young person of Ayr
　　Whose head was remarkably square;
　　　On the top, in fine weather,
　　　She wore a gold feather –
　　Which dazzled the people of Ayr.

TWENTY-SIX NONSENSE
RHYMES AND PICTURES

1.   The absolutely abstemious Ass,
who resided in a barrel and only lived on
soda water and pickled cucumbers.

2.   The bountiful Beetle,
who always carried a green umbrella when it didn't rain
and left it at home when it did.

3.   The comfortable confidential Cow,
who sat in her red morocco armchair and
toasted her own bread at the parlour fire.

4.   The dolomphious Duck,
who caught spotted frogs for her dinner
with a runcible spoon.

5.   The enthusiastic Elephant,
who ferried himself across the water with the
kitchen poker and a new pair of earrings.

6.   The fizzgiggious Fish,
      who always walked about upon stilts,
      because he had no legs.

7.   The good-natured grey Gull,
      who carried the old owl and his crimson carpet bag
      across the river, because he could not swim.

8.   The hasty higgeldipiggledy Hen,
     who went to market in a blue bonnet and shawl,
     and bought a fish for her supper.

9.   The inventive Indian,
     who caught a remarkable rabbit in a
     stupendous silver spoon.

10. The judicious jubilant Jay,
who did up her back hair every morning with a wreath of r
three feathers and a gold pin.

11. The kicking Kangaroo,
who wore a pale-pink muslin dress
with blue spots.

12. The lively learned Lobster,
who mended his own clothes with
a needle and thread.

13. The melodious meritorious Mouse,
who played a merry minuet on the
pianoforte.

14. The nutritious Newt,
who purchased a round plum pudding
for his granddaughter.

15. The obsequious ornamental Ostrich,
who bore boots to keep his
feet quite dry.

16. The perpendicular purple Polly,
who read the newspaper and ate parsnip pie
with his spectacles.

17. The queer querulous quail,
who smoked a pipe of tobacco on the top of
a tin tea kettle.

18.   The rural runcible Raven,
      who wore a white wig and flew away
      with the carpet broom.

19.   The scroobious Snake,
      who always wore a hat on his head, for
      fear he should bite anybody.

20. The tumultuous tom-tommy Tortoise,
who beat a drum all day long in the
middle of the wilderness.

21. The umbrageous Umbrella-maker,
whose face nobody ever saw, because it was
always covered by his umbrella.

22. The visibly vicious Vulture,
who wrote some verses to a veal cutlet in a
volume bound in vellum.

23. The worrying whizzing Wasp,
who stood on a table and played sweetly on a
flute with a morning cap.

24. The excellent double-extra-XX-
    imbibing King Xerxes, who lived a
    long while ago.

25. The Yonghy-Bonghy-Bò,
    whose head was ever so much bigger than his
    body, and whose hat was rather small.

26.   The zigzag zealous Zebra,
who carried five Monkeys on his back all
the way to Jellibolee.

LAUGHABLE LYRICS

THE DONG WITH A LUMINOUS NOSE

When awful darkness and silence reign
Over the great Gromboolian plain
   Through the long, long wintry nights;
When the angry breakers roar
As they beat on the rocky shore;
   When storm clouds brood on the towering heights
Of the hills of the Chankly Bore –

Then, through the vast and gloomy dark
There moves what seems a fiery spark,
   A lonely spark with silvery rays
     Piercing the coal-black night,
     A meteor strange and bright;
   Hither and thither the vision strays,
     A single lurid light.

Slowly it wanders, pauses, creeps –
Anon it sparkles, flashes and leaps,
And ever as onward it gleaming goes,
A light on the bong-tree stems it throws.

And those who watch at that midnight hour
From hall or terrace or lofty tower
Cry, as the wild light passes along,
    "The Dong! The Dong!
  The wandering Dong through the forest goes!
      The Dong! The Dong!
  The Dong with a luminous nose!"

    Long years ago
    The Dong was happy and gay,
Till he fell in love with a Jumbly girl
    Who came to those shores one day.
For the Jumblies came in a sieve, they did,
Landing at eve near the Zemmery Fidd,
    Where the oblong oysters grow
    And the rocks are smooth and grey.
And all the woods and the valleys rang
With the chorus they daily and nightly sang –
        "Far and few, far and few,
        Are the lands where the Jumblies live;
        Their heads are green, and their hands are blue,
        And they went to sea in a sieve."

Happily, happily passed those days,
    While the cheerful Jumblies stayed!
    They danced in circlets all night long,
    To the plaintive pipe of the lively Dong,
    In moonlight, shine or shade.
For day and night he was always there
By the side of the Jumbly girl so fair,
With her sky-blue hands and her sea-green hair;
Till the morning came of that hateful day
When the Jumblies sailed in their sieve away,
And the Dong was left on the cruel shore
Gazing, gazing for evermore –
Ever keeping his weary eyes on

That pea-green sail on the far horizon –
Singing the Jumbly chorus still
As he sat all day on the grassy hill:
      "Far and few, far and few,
         Are the lands where the Jumblies live;
         Their heads are green, and their hands are blue,
            And they went to sea in a sieve."

But when the sun was low in the west,
      The Dong arose and said,
"What little sense I once possessed
      Has quite gone out of my head!"
And since that day he wanders still
By lake and forest, marsh and hill,
Singing, "Oh, somewhere, in valley or plain,
Might I find my Jumbly girl again!
For ever I'll seek by lake and shore
Till I find my Jumbly girl once more!"

      Playing a pipe with silvery squeaks,
      Since then his Jumbly girl he seeks;
      And because by night he could not see,
      He gathered the bark of the twangum tree
         On the flowery plain that grows.
         And he wove him a wondrous nose –
      A nose as strange as a nose could be!
Of vast proportions and painted red,
And tied with cords to the back of his head.
      In a hollow rounded space it ended
      With a luminous lamp within suspended,
         All fenced about
         With a bandage stout
      To prevent the wind from blowing it out;
And with holes all round to send the light
In gleaming rays on the dismal night.

And now each night, and all night long,
Over those plains still roams the Dong;
And above the wail of the chimp and snipe
You may hear the squeak of his plaintive pipe,
While ever he seeks, but seeks in vain,
To meet with his Jumbly girl again;
Lonely and wild, all night he goes,
The Dong with a luminous nose!
And all who watch at the midnight hour
From Hall or Terrace or lofty Tower
Cry, as they trace the meteor bright
Moving along through the dreary night,

    "This is the hour when forth he goes,
    The Dong with a luminous nose!
    Yonder, over the plain he goes –
      He goes!
      He goes! –
    The Dong with a luminous nose!"

THE TWO OLD BACHELORS

Two old bachelors were living in one house;
One caught a muffin, the other caught a mouse.
Said he who caught the muffin to him who caught the mouse,
"This happens just in time! For we've nothing in the house
Save a tiny slice of lemon and a teaspoonful of honey –
And what to do for dinner, since we haven't any money?
And what can we expect, if we haven't any dinner,
But to lose our teeth and eyelashes and keep on growing thinner?"

Said he who caught the mouse to him who caught the muffin,
"We might cook this little mouse, if we only had some stuffin'!
If we had but sage and onion, we could do extremely well;
But how to get that stuffin' it is difficult to tell!"

Those two old bachelors ran quickly to the town
And asked for sage and onion as they wandered up and down;
They borrowed two large onions, but no sage was to be found
In the shops or in the market, or in all the gardens round.

But someone said, "A hill there is, a little to the north,
And to its purpledicular top a narrow way leads forth;

And there, among the rugged rocks, abides an ancient sage –
An earnest man who reads all day a most perplexing page.
Climb up and seize him by the toes – all studious as he sits –
And pull him down, and chop him into endless little bits!
Then mix him with your onion (cut up likewise into scraps),
When your stuffin' will be ready, and very good – perhaps."

Those two old bachelors without loss of time
The nearly purpledicular crags at once began to climb;
And at the top, among the rocks, all seated in a nook,
They saw that sage a-reading of a most enormous book.

"You earnest sage," aloud they cried, "your book you've read enough in!
We wish to chop you into bits to mix you into stuffin'!"

But that old sage looked calmly up and, with his awful book,
At those two bachelors' bald heads a certain aim he took;
And over crag and precipice they rolled promiscuous down –
At once they rolled, and never stopped in lane or field or town;
And when they reached their house, they found (besides their want of stuff)
The mouse had fled – and, previously, had eaten up the muffin.

They left their home in silence by the once convivial door,
And from that hour those bachelors were never heard of more.

THE PELICAN CHORUS

King and queen of the pelicans we –
No other birds so grand we see!
None but we have feet like fins!
With lovely leathery throats and chins!
    Ploffskin, pluffskin, pelican jee!
    We think no birds so happy as we!
    Plumpskin, ploshkin, pelican jill!
    We think so then, and we thought so still!

We live on the Nile. The Nile we love.
By night we sleep on the cliffs above;
By day we fish, and at eve we stand
On long bare islands of yellow sand.
And when the sun sinks slowly down,
And the great rock walls grow dark and brown,
Where the purple river rolls fast and dim
And the ivory ibis starlike skim,
Wing to wing we dance around,
Stamping our feet with a flumpy sound,

Opening our mouths as pelicans ought –
And this is the song we nightly snort:
    Ploffskin, pluffskin, pelican jee!
    We think no birds so happy as we!
    Plumpskin, ploshkin, pelican jill!
    We think so then, and we thought so still!

Last year came out our daughter Dell,
And all the birds received her well.
To do her honour a feast we made
For every bird that can swim or wade –
Herons and gulls, and cormorants black,
Cranes, and Flamingoes with scarlet back,
Plovers and storks, and geese in clouds,
Swans and dilberry ducks in crowds –
Thousands of birds in wondrous flight!
They ate and drank and danced all night,
And echoing back from the rocks you heard
Multitude echoes from bird and bird –
    Ploffskin, pluffskin, pelican jee!
    We think no birds so happy as we!
    Plumpskin, ploshkin, pelican jill!
    We think so then, and we thought so still!

Yes, they came – and, among the rest,
The king of the cranes, all grandly dressed.
Such a lovely tail! Its feathers float
Between the ends of his blue dress coat;
With pea-green trousers all so neat,
And a delicate frill to hide his feet
(For though no one speaks of it, everyone knows
He has got no webs between his toes).

As soon as he saw our daughter Dell,
In violent love that crane king fell,
On seeing her waddling form so fair,
With a wreath of shrimps in her short white hair.
And, before the end of the next long day,

Our Dell had given her heart away;
For the king of the cranes had won that heart
With a crocodile's egg and a large fish tart.
She vowed to marry the king of the cranes,
Leaving the Nile for stranger plains;
And away they flew in a gathering crowd
Of endless birds in a lengthening cloud.
    Ploffskin, pluffskin, pelican jee!
    We think no birds so happy as we!
    Plumpskin, ploshkin, pelican jill!
    We think so then, and we thought so still!

And far away in the twilight sky
We heard them singing a lessening cry –
Farther and farther, till out of sight,
And we stood alone in the silent night!
Often since, in the nights of June,
We sit on the sand and watch the moon –
She has gone to the great Gromboolian plain,
And we probably never shall meet again!
Oft, in the long still nights of June,
We sit on the rocks and watch the moon –
She dwells by the streams of the Chankly Bore.
And we probably never shall see her more.
    Ploffskin, pluffskin, pelican jee!
    We think no birds so happy as we!
    Plumpskin, ploshkin, pelican jill!
    We think so then, and we thought so still!

NOTE: The air of this and the following song by Edward Lear; the arrangement for the piano by Professor Pomè, of Sanremo, Italy.

THE PELICANS.

King and Queen of the Peli-cans we, No other birds so grand we see!

None but we have feet like fins with love-ly lea-the-ry throats and chins,

Coro—piu sostenuto.

Ploff-skin, Pluff-skin, Pe-li-can Jee! we think no birds so hap-py as we!

Plump-skin, Ploff-skin, Pe-li-can Jill! We think so then, and we thought so still!

THE COURTSHIP OF THE
YONGHY-BONGHY-BÒ

I

On the Coast of Coromandel,
 Where the early pumpkins blow,
  In the middle of the woods
  Lived the Yonghy-Bonghy-Bò.
Two old chairs, and half a candle,
One old jug without a handle –
  These were all his worldly goods;
  In the middle of the woods
  These were all the worldly goods
  Of the Yonghy-Bonghy-Bò,
  Of the Yonghy-Bonghy-Bò.

II

Once, among the bong trees walking,
 Where the early pumpkins blow,
  To a little heap of stones
  Came the Yonghy-Bonghy-Bò.

There he heard a lady talking
To some milk-white hens of Dorking –
    "'Tis the Lady Jingly Jones!
    On that little heap of stones
    Sits the Lady Jingly Jones!"
Said the Yonghy-Bonghy-Bò,
Said the Yonghy-Bonghy-Bò.

III

"Lady Jingly! Lady Jingly,
    Sitting where the pumpkins blow,
        Will you come and be my wife?"
    Said the Yonghy-Bonghy-Bò.
"I am tired of living singly –
On this coast so wild and shingly –
        I'm a-weary of my life;
        If you'll come and be my wife,
        Quite serene would be my life!"
    Said the Yonghy-Bonghy-Bò,
    Said the Yonghy-Bonghy-Bò.

IV

On this Coast of Coromandel
    Shrimps and watercresses grow,
        Prawns are plentiful and cheap,"
    Said the Yonghy-Bonghy-Bò.
"You shall have my chairs and candle,
And my jug without a handle!
        Gaze upon the rolling deep
        (Fish is plentiful and cheap) –
        As the sea, my love is deep!"
    Said the Yonghy-Bonghy-Bò,
    Said the Yonghy-Bonghy-Bò.

V

Lady Jingly answered sadly,
　　And her tears began to flow,
　　　"Your proposal comes too late,
　　Mr Yonghy-Bonghy-Bò!
I would be your wife most gladly!"
(Here she twirled her fingers madly)
　　　"But in England I've a mate!
　　　Yes! You've asked me far too late,
　　　For in England I've a mate!
　　Mr Yonghy-Bonghy-Bò!
　　Mr Yonghy-Bonghy-Bò!

VI

"Mr Jones (his name is Handel –
　　Handel Jones, Esquire, & Co.)
　　　Dorking fowls delights to send,
　　Mr Yonghy-Bonghy-Bò!
Keep, oh, keep your chairs and candle,
And your jug without a handle –
　　　I can merely be your friend!
　　　Should my Jones more Dorkings send,
　　　I will give you three, my friend!
　　Mr Yonghy-Bonghy-Bò!
　　Mr Yonghy-Bonghy-Bò!

VII

"Though you've such a tiny body,
　　And your head so large doth grow;
　　　Though your hat may blow away,
　　Mr Yonghy-Bonghy-Bò;
Though you're such a hoddy-doddy,
Yet I wish that I could modi-
　　　Fy the words I needs must say!
　　　Will you please to go away?
　　　That is all I have to say,
　　Mr Yonghy-Bonghy-Bò!
　　Mr Yonghy-Bonghy-Bò!

VIII

Down the slippery slopes of Myrtle,
Where the early pumpkins blow,
To the calm and silent sea
Fled the Yonghy-Bonghy-Bò.
There, beyond the Bay of Gurtle,
Lay a large and lively turtle.
"You're the cove," he said, "for me;
On your back beyond the sea,
Turtle, you shall carry me!"
Said the Yonghy-Bonghy-Bò,
Said the Yonghy-Bonghy-Bò.

IX

Through the silent-roaring ocean
Did the turtle swiftly go;
Holding fast upon his shell
Rode the Yonghy-Bonghy-Bò.
With a sad primeval motion
Towards the sunset isles of Boshen
Still the turtle bore him well.
Holding fast upon his shell,
"Lady Jingly Jones, farewell!"
Sang the Yonghy-Bonghy-Bò,
Sang the Yonghy-Bonghy-Bò.

X

From the Coast of Coromandel
    Did that lady never go;
        On that heap of stones she mourns
    For the Yonghy-Bonghy-Bò.
On that Coast of Coromandel,
In his jug without a handle,
        Still she weeps and daily moans;
        On that little heap of stones
        To her Dorking hens she moans,
    For the Yonghy-Bonghy-Bò,
    For the Yonghy-Bonghy-Bò.

THE YONGHY BONGHY BÒ.

THE POBBLE WHO HAS NO TOES

I

The Pobble who has not toes
  Had once as many as we;
When they said, "Some day you may lose them all"
  He replied, "Fish fiddle de-dee!"
And his aunt Jobiska made him drink
Lavender water tinged with pink;
For she said, "The world in general knows
There's nothing so good for a Pobble's toes!"

II

The Pobble who has no toes
  Swam across the Bristol Channel;
But, before he set out, he wrapped his nose
  In a piece of scarlet flannel;
For his aunt Jobiska said, "No harm
Can come to his toes if his nose is warm;
And it's perfectly known that a Pobble's toes
Are safe – provided he minds his nose."

III

The Pobble swam fast and well,
   And when boats or ships came near him,
He tinkledy-binkledy-winkled a bell
   So that all the world could hear him.
And all the sailors and admirals cried,
When they saw him nearing the farther side,
"He has gone to fish, for his aunt Jobiska's
Runcible cat with crimson whiskers!"

IV

But before he touched the shore –
   The shore of the Bristol Channel –
A sea-green porpoise carried away
   His wrapper of scarlet flannel.
And when he came to observe his feet,
Formerly garnished with toes so neat,
His face at once became forlorn
On perceiving that all his toes were gone!

V

And nobody ever knew,
   From that dark day to the present,
Whoso had taken the Pobble's toes,
   In a manner so far from pleasant.
Whether the shrimps or crawfish grey,
Or crafty mermaids stole them away,
Nobody knew – and nobody knows
How the Pobble was robbed of his twice five toes!

VI

The Pobble who has no toes
   Was placed in a friendly bark,
And they rowed him back, and carried him up
   To his aunt Jobiska's park.
And she made him a feast, at his earnest wish,
Of eggs and buttercups fried with fish;
And she said, "It's a fact the whole world knows
That Pobbles are happier without their toes."

THE NEW VESTMENTS

There lived an old man in the Kingdom of Tess,
Who invented a purely original dress;
And when it was perfectly made and complete,
He opened the door and walked into the street.

By way of a hat, he'd a loaf of brown bread,
In the middle of which he inserted his head;
His shirt was made up of no end of dead mice,
The warmth of whose skins was quite fluffy and nice;
His drawers were of rabbit skins – so were his shoes;
His stockings were skins, but it is not known whose;
His waistcoat and trousers were made of pork chops;
His buttons where jujubes and chocolate drops;
His coat was all pancakes, with jam for a border,
And a girdle of biscuits to keep it in order;
And he wore over all, as a screen from bad weather,
A cloak of green cabbage leaves stitched all together.

He had walked a short way when he heard a great noise,
Of all sorts of beasticles, birdlings and boys;
And from every long street and dark lane in the town
Beasts, birdles and boys in a tumult rushed down.

Two cows and a calf ate his cabbage-leaf cloak;
Four apes seized his girdle, which vanished like smoke;
Three kids ate up half of his pancaky coat,
And the tails were devoured by an ancient he-goat;
An army of dogs in a twinkling tore *up* his
Pork waistcoat and trousers to give to their puppies;
And while they were growling and mumbling the chops,
Ten boys prigged the jujubes and chocolate drops.
He tried to run back to his house, but in vain,
For scores of fat pigs came again and again:
They rushed out of stables and hovels and doors;
They tore off his stockings, his shoes and his drawers;
And now from the housetops with screechings descend
Striped, spotted, white, black and grey cats without end –
They jumped on his shoulders and knocked off his hat,
When crows, ducks and hens made a mincemeat of that;
They speedily flew at his sleeves in a trice,
And utterly tore up his shirt of dead mice;
They swallowed the last of his shirt with a squall –
Whereon he ran home with no clothes on at all.

And he said to himself, as he bolted the door,
"I will not wear a similar dress any more,
Any more, any more, any more, never more!"

MR AND MRS DISCOBBOLOS

I

Mr and Mrs Discobbolos
    Climbed to the top of a wall.
    And they sat to watch the sunset sky,
    And to hear the nupiter piffkin cry,
        And the biscuit buffalo call.
They took up a roll and some camomile tea,
And both were as happy as happy could be,
        Till Mrs Discobbolos said,
        "Oh! W! X! Y! Z!
        It has just come into my head —
        Suppose we should happen to fall!!!!!
            Darling Mr Discobbolos!

II

"Suppose we should fall down flumpetty,
        Just like pieces of stone,
    Onto the thorns, or into the moat —
    What would become of your new green coat?
        And might you not break a bone?
It never occurred to me before,

That perhaps we shall never go down any more!"
    And Mrs Discobbolos said,
    "Oh! W! X! Y! Z!
    What put it into your head
    To climb up this wall, my own
        Darling Mr Discobbolos?"

III

Mr Discobbolos answered,
    "At first it gave me pain,
    And I felt my ears turn perfectly pink
    When your exclamation made me think
    We might never get down again!
But now I believe it is wiser far
To remain for ever just where we are."
    And Mr Discobbolos said,
    "Oh! W! X! Y! Z!
    It has just come into my head –
    We shall never go down again,
        Dearest Mrs Discobbolos!"

IV

So Mr and Mrs Discobbolos
    Stood up and began to sing,
    "Far away from hurry and strife,
    Here we will pass the rest of life,
    Ding a dong, ding dong, ding!
We want no knives nor forks nor chairs,
No tables nor carpets nor household cares;
    From worry of life we've fled –
    Oh! W! X! Y! Z!
    There is no more trouble ahead,
    Sorrow or any such thing,
        For Mr and Mrs Discobbolos!"

THE QUANGLE-WANGLE'S HAT

I

On the top of the crumpetty tree
  The Quangle-Wangle sat,
But his face you could not see,
  On account of his beaver hat.
For his hat was a hundred and two feet wide,
With ribbons and bibbons on every side,
And bells, and buttons, and loops, and lace,
So that nobody ever could see the face
      Of the Quangle-Wangle-Quee.

II

The Quangle-Wangle said
  To himself on the crumpetty tree,
"Jam and jelly and bread
  Are the best of food for me!
But the longer I live on this crumpetty tree,
The plainer than ever it seems to me
That very few people come this way,
And that life on the whole is far from gay!"
      Said the Quangle-Wangle-Quee.

III

But there came to the crumpetty tree
   Mr and Mrs Canary;
And they said, "Did ever you see
   Any spot so charmingly airy?
May we build a nest on your lovely hat?
Mr Quangle-Wangle, grant us that!
Oh please, let us come and build a nest
Of whatever material suits you best,
       Mr Quangle-Wangle-Quee!"

IV

And besides, to the crumpetty tree
   Came the stork, the duck and the owl,
The snail and the bumblebee,
   The frog and the fimble fowl
(The fimble fowl, with a corkscrew leg) –
And all of them said, "We humbly beg
We may build our homes on your lovely hat –
Mr Quangle-Wangle, grant us that!
       Mr Quangle-Wangle-Quee!"

V

And the golden grouse came there,
   And the Pobble who has no toes,
And the small olympian bear,
   And the Dong with a luminous nose,
And the blue baboon, who played the flute,
And the orient calf from the Land of Tute,
And the attery squash, and the bisky bat –
All came and built on the lovely hat
       Of the Quangle-Wangle-Quee.

VI

And the Quangle-Wangle said
  To himself on the crumpetty tree,
"When all these creatures move,
  What a wonderful noise there'll be!"
And at night, by the light of the mulberry moon,
They danced to the flute of the blue baboon,
On the broad green leaves of the crumpetty tree,
And all were as happy as happy could be,
      With the Quangle-Wangle-Quee.

THE CUMMERBUND

AN INDIAN POEM

I

She sat upon her dobie,
  To watch the evening star,
And all the punkahs, as they passed,
  Cried, "My, how fair you are!"
Around her bower, with quivering leaves,
  The tall kamsamahs grew,
And kitmutgars in wild festoons
  Hung down from tchokis blue.

II

Below her home the river rolled
  With soft meloobious sound,
Where golden-finned chuprassies swam,
  In myriads circling round.
Above, on tallest trees remote,
  Green ayahs perched alone,
And all night long the mussak moaned
  Its melancholy tone.

III

And where the purple nullahs threw
   Their branches far and wide,
And silvery goreewallahs flew
   In silence, side by side,
The little bheesties' twittering cry
   Rose on the flagrant air,
And oft the angry jampan howled
   Deep in his hateful lair.

IV

She sat upon her dobie,
   She heard the nimmak hum,
When all at once a cry arose,
   "The Cummerbund is come!"
In vain she fled – with open jaws
   The angry monster followed,
And so (before assistance came)
   That lady fair was swallowed.

V

They sought in vain for even a bone
   Respectfully to bury;
They said, "Hers was a dreadful fate!"
   (And echo answered, "Very.")
They nailed her dobie to the wall,
   Where last her form was seen,
And underneath they wrote these words,
   In yellow, blue and green:

"Beware, ye fair! Ye fair, beware!
   Nor sit out late at night,
Lest horrid Cummerbunds should come
   And swollow you outright."

NOTE: First published in *Times of India*, Bombay, July 1874.

THE AKOND OF SWAT

Who, or why, or which, or *what*   is the Akond of Swat?

Is he tall or short, or dark or fair?
Does he sit on a stool or a sofa or chair,   or SQUAT,
                    the Akond of Swat?

Is he wise or foolish, young or old?
Does he drink his soup and his coffee cold,   or HOT,
                    the Akond of Swat?

Does he sing or whistle, jabber or talk,
And when riding abroad does he gallop or walk,   or TROT,
                    the Akond of Swat?

Does he wear a turban, a fez or a hat?
Does he sleep on a mattress, a bed or a mat,   or a COT,
                    the Akond of Swat?

When he writes a copy in round-hand size,
Does he cross his t's and finish his i's   with a DOT,
                    the Akond of Swat?

Can he write a letter concisely clear
Without a speck or a smudge or smear   or BLOT,
                    the Akond of Swat?

Do his people like him extremely well?
Or do they, whenever they can, rebel,   or PLOT,
                    at the Akond of Swat?

If he catches them then, either old or young,
Does he have them chopped in pieces or hung,
                                      or *shot*,
                                  the Akond of Swat?

Do his people prig in the lanes or park?
Or even at times, when days are dark,
                                  GARROTTE?
                              Oh, the Akond of Swat!

Does he study the wants of his own dominion?
Or doesn't he care for public opinion
                                      a JOT,
                                  the Akond of Swat?

To amuse his mind do his people show him
Pictures, or anyone's last new poem,
                                  or WHAT,
                              for the Akond of Swat?

At night, if he suddenly screams and wakes,
Do they bring him only a few small cakes,
                                  or a LOT,
                              for the Akond of Swat?

Does he live on turnips, tea or tripe?
Does he like his shawl to be marked with a stripe   or a DOT,
                                  the Akond of Swat?

Does he like to lie on his back in a boat,
Like the lady who lived in that isle remote,
                                  SHALOTT,
                                  the Akond of Swat?

Is he quiet, or always making a fuss?
Is his steward a Swiss or a Swede or a Russ,
                                  or a SCOT,
                                  the Akond of Swat?

Does he like to sit by the calm blue wave?
Or to sleep and snore in a dark green cave,
                                  or a GROT,
                                  the Akond of Swat?

Does he drink small beer from a silver jug,
Or a bowl, or a glass, or a cup, or a mug,
                                  or a POT,
                                  the Akond of Swat?

Does he beat his wife with a gold-topped pipe,
When she lets the gooseberries grow too ripe,
                                  or ROT,
                                  the Akond of Swat?

Does he wear a white tie when he dines with friends,
And tie it neat in a bow with ends,
                                  or a KNOT,
                                  the Akond of Swat?

Does he like new cream and hate mince pies?
When he looks at the sun, does he wink his eyes   or NOT,
                                                        the Akond of Swat?

Does he teach his subjects to roast and bake?
Does he sail about on an inland lake   in a YACHT,
                                                        the Akond of Swat?

Someone, or nobody, knows I wot
Who or which or why or what

                                                        is the Akond of Swat!

NOTE: For the existence of this potentate, see Indian newspapers, passim. The proper way to read the verses is to make an immense emphasis on the monosyllabic rhymes, which indeed ought to be shouted out by a chorus.

NONSENSE COOKERY,
BOTANY AND ALPHABETS

NONSENSE COOKERY

Extract from *The Nonsense Gazette* for August 1870

Our readers will be interested in the following communications from our valued and learned contributor, Prof. Bosh, whose labours in the fields of culinary and botanical science are so well known to all the world. The first three articles richly merit to be added to the domestic cookery of every family – those which follow claim the attention of all botanists; and we are happy to be able, through Dr Bosh's kindness, to present our readers with illustrations of his discoveries. All the new flowers are found in the Valley of Verrikwier, near the Lake of Oddgrow, and on the summit of the hill Orfeltugg.

THREE RECEIPTS FOR DOMESTIC COOKERY

TO MAKE AND AMBLONGUS PIE

Take 4 pounds (say 4½ pounds) of fresh amblongusses, and put them in a small pipkin.

Cover them with water and boil them for 8 hours incessantly; after which, add 2 pints of new milk, and proceed to boil for 4 hours more.

When you have ascertained that the amblongusses are quite soft, take them out and place them in a wide pan, taking care to shake them well previously.

Grate some nutmeg over the surface, and cover them carefully with powdered gingerbread, curry powder and a sufficient quantity of cayenne pepper.

Remove the pan into the next room and place it on the floor. Bring it back again, and let it simmer for three quarters of an hour. Shake the pan violently till all the amblongusses have become of a pale purple colour.

Then, having prepared the paste, insert the whole carefully, adding at the same time a small pigeon, 2 slices of beef, 4 cauliflowers and any number of oysters.

Watch patiently till the crust begins to rise, and add a pinch of salt from time to time.

Serve up in a clean dish, and throw the whole out of window as fast as possible.

TO MAKE CRUMBOBBLIOUS CUTLETS

Procure some strips of beef, and, having cut them into the smallest possible slices, proceed to cut them still smaller – eight, or perhaps nine times.

When the whole is thus minced, brush it up hastily with a new clothes brush and stir round rapidly and capriciously with a salt spoon or a soup ladle.

Place the whole in a saucepan and remove it to a sunny place – say the roof of the house, if free from sparrows or other birds – and leave it there for about a week.

At the end of that time, add a little lavender, some oil of almonds and a few herring bones; and then cover the whole with 4 gallons of clarified crumbobblious sauce, when it will be ready for use.

Cut it into the shape of ordinary cutlets, and serve up in a clean tablecloth or dinner napkin.

TO MAKE GOSKY PATTIES

Take a pig three or four years of age and tie him by the off hind leg to a post. Place 5 pounds of currants, 3 of sugar, 2 pecks of peas, 18 roast chestnuts, a candle and 6 bushels of turnips within his reach; if he eats these, constantly provide him with more.

Then procure some cream, some slices of Cheshire cheese, 4 quires of foolscap paper and a packet of black pins. Work the whole into a paste, and spread it out to dry on a sheet of clean brown waterproof linen.

When the paste is perfectly dry, but not before, proceed to beat the pig violently with the handle of a large broom. If he squeals, beat him again.

Visit the paste and beat the pig alternately for some days, and ascertain if, at the end of that period, the whole is about to turn into gosky patties.

If it does not then, it never will – and in that case the pig may be let loose, and the whole process may be considered as finished.

NONSENSE BOTANY

1.1. Baccopipia Gracilis   1.2. Bottlephorkia Spoonifolia

1.3. Cockatooca Superba

1.4. Fishia Marina

1.5. Guittara Pensilis

1.6. Manypeeplia Upsidownia

1.7. Phattfacia Stupenda

1.8. Piggiwiggia Pyramidalis

1.9. Plumbunnia Nutritiosa

1.10. Pollybirdia Singularis

2.1. Barkia Howlaloudia

2.2. Enkoopia Chickabiddia

2.3. Jinglia Tinkettlia

2.4. Nasticreechia Krorluppia

2.5. Arthbroomia Rigida

2.6. Sophtsluggia Glutinosa

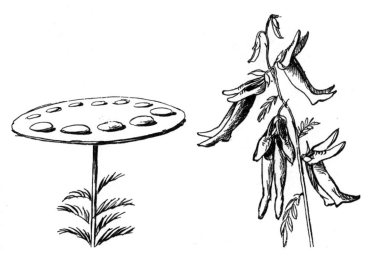

2.7. Minspysia Deliciosa

2.8. Shoebootia Utilis

2.9. Stunnia Dinnerbellia

2.10. Tickia Orologica

2.11. Washtubbia Circularis

2.12. Tigerlillia Terribilis

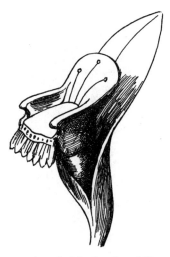

3.1. Armchairia Comfortabilis

3.2. Bassia Palealensis

3.3. Bubblia Blowpipia

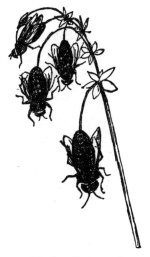

3.4. Bluebottlia Buzztilentia

3.5. Crabbia Horrida

3.6. Smalltoothcombia Domestica

3.7. Knutmigrata Simplice

3.8. Tureenia Ladlecum

3.9. Puffia Leatherbéllowsa   3.10.   Queeriflora Babyöides

NONSENSE ALPHABETS

A

1a. A was an ant
Who seldom stood still,
And who made a nice house
In the side of a hill.

a

Nice little ant!

1c. A was an ape
Who stole some white tape
And tied up his toes
In four beautiful bows.

a

Funny old ape!

1b. A was once an apple pie,
Pidy,
Widy,
Tidy,
Pidy,
Nice insidy,
Apple pie!

1d. A was an area arch
Where washerwomen sat;
They made a lot of lovely starch
To starch Papa's cravat.

B

2a. **B** was a book
With a binding of blue
And pictures and stories
For me and for you.

b

Nice little book!

2c. **B** was a bat
Who slept all the day
And fluttered about
When the sun went away.

b

Brown little bat!

2b. **B** was once a little bear,
Beary,
Wary,
Hairy,
Beary,
Taky cary,
Little bear!

2d. **B** was a bottle blue
Which was not very small;
Papa, he filled it full of beer,
And then he drank it all.

C

3a.   C was a cat
Who ran after a rat;
But his courage did fail
When she seized on his tail.

C
Crafty old cat!

3c.   C was a camel:
You rode on his hump;
And if you fell off,
You came down such a bump!

C
What a high camel!

3b.   C was once a little cake,
Caky,
Baky,
Maky,
Caky,
Taky caky,
Little cake!

3d.   C was Papa's grey cat,
Who caught a squeaky mouse;
She pulled him by his twirly tail
All about the house.

D

4a. D was a duck
With spots on his back,
Who lived in the water
And always said "Quack!"

d
Dear little duck!

4c. D was a dove
Who lived in a wood,
With such pretty soft wings
And so gentle and good!

d
Dear little dove!

4b. D was once a little doll,
Dolly,
Molly,
Polly,
Nolly,
Nursy dolly,
Little doll!

4d. D was Papa's white duck,
Who had a curly tail;
One day it ate a great fat frog,
Besides a leetle snail.

E

5a. E was an elephant,
Stately and wise:
He had tusks and a trunk,
And two queer little eyes.

e
Oh, what funny small eyes!

5c. E was an eagle
Who sat on the rocks
And looked down on the fields
And the faraway flocks.

e
Beautiful eagle!

5b. E was once a little eel,
Eely,
Weely,
Peely,
Eely,
Twirly, tweely,
Little eel!

5d. E was a little egg
Upon the breakfast table;
Papa came in and ate it up
As fast as he was able.

F

6a. F was a fish
Who was caught in a net;
But he got out again,
And is quite alive yet.

f

Lively young fish!

6c. F was a fan
made of beautiful stuff –
And when it was used,
It went puffy-puff-puff.

f

Nice little fan!

6b. F was once a little fish,
Fishy,
Wishy,
Squishy,
Fishy,
In a dishy,
Little fish!

6d. F was a little fish.
Cook in the river took it.
Papa said, "Cook, cook, bring a dis
And, cook, be quick and cook

G

7a. **G** was a goat
Who was spotted with brown:
When he did not lie still,
He walked up and down.

g
Good little goat!

7c. **G** was a gooseberry
Perfectly red –
To be made into jam
And eaten with bread.

g
Gooseberry red!

7b. **G** was once a little goose,
Goosy,
Moosy,
Boosey,
Goosey,
Waddly-woosy,
Little goose!

7d. **G** was Papa's new gun;
He put it in a box,
And then he went and bought a bun
And walked about the Docks.

H

8a. H was a hat
Which was all on one side;
Its crown was too high,
And its brim was too wide.
h
Oh, what a hat!

8c. H was a heron
Who stood in a stream:
The length of his neck
And his legs was extreme.
h
Long-legged heron!

8b. H was once a little hen,
    Henny,
    Chenny,
    Tenny,
    Henny,
    Eggsy-any,
    Little hen?

8d. H was Papa's new hat;
    He wore it on his head:
Outside it was completely black,
    But inside it was red.

I

9a. I was some ice,
So white and so nice,
But which nobody tasted –
And so it was wasted.

i
All that good ice!

9c. I was an inkstand
Which stood on a table,
With a nice pen to write with
When we are able.

i
Neat little inkstand!

9b. I was once a bottle of ink,
Inky,
Dinky,
Thinky,
Inky,
Blacky minky,
Bottle of ink!

9d. I was an inkstand new;
Papa, he likes to use it;
He keeps it in his pocket now,
For fear that he should lose it.

J

10a. J was a jackdaw
Who hopped up and down
In the principal street
Of a neighbouring town.

j

All through the town!

10c. J was a jug,
So pretty and white,
With fresh water in it
At morning and night.

j

Nice little jug!

10b. J was once a jar of jam,
Jammy,
Mammy,
Clammy,
Jammy,
Sweety, swammy,
Jar of jam!

10d. J was some apple jam,
of which Papa ate part;
But all the rest he took away
And stuffed into a tart.

K

11a. K was a kite
      Which flew out of sight,
      Above houses so high,
      Quite into the sky.

          k
      Fly away, kite!

11c. K was a kingfisher:
      Quickly he flew,
      So bright and so pretty –
      Green, purple and blue!

          k
      Kingfisher blue!

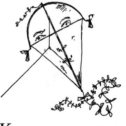

11b. K was once a little kite,
              Kity,
              Whity,
              Flighty,
              Kity,
          Out of sighty,
          Little kite!

11d. K was a great new kite;
          Papa, he saw it fly
      Above a thousand chimney pots
          And all about the sky.

L

12a. L was a light
Which burned all the night
And lighted the gloom
Of a very dark room.

l

Useful nice light!

12c. L was a lily,
So white and so sweet!
To see it and smell it
Was quite a nice treat.

l

Beautiful lily!

12b. L was once a little lark,
Larky,
Marky,
Harky,
Larky,
In the parky,
Little lark!

12d. L was a fine new lamp;
But, when the wick was lit,
Papa, he said, "This light ain't go
I cannot read a bit!"

M

13a. M was a mill
Which stood on a hill
And turned round and round
With a loud hummy sound.

m
Useful old mill!

13c. M was a man
Who walked round and round –
And he wore a long coat
That came down to the ground.

m
Funny old man!

13b. M was once a little mouse,
Mousy,
Bousy,
Sousy,
Mousy,
In the housy,
Little mouse!

13d. M was a dish of mince;
It looked so good to eat!
Papa, he quickly ate it up
And said, "This is a treat!"

N

14a. N was a net
Which was thrown in the sea
To catch fish for dinner
For you and for me.

n
Nice little net!

14c. N was a nut,
So smooth and so brown!
And when it was ripe,
It fell tumble-dum-down.

n
Nice little nut!

14b. N was once a little needle,
Needly,
Tweedly,
Threedly,
Needly,
Wisky, wheedly,
Little needle!

14d. N was a nut that grew
High up upon a tree;
Papa, who could not reach it, said
"That's *much* too high for me!"

O

15a. O was an orange
So yellow and round:
When it fell off the tree,
It felll down to the ground.

O
Down to the ground!

15c. O was an oyster
Who lived in his shell:
If you let him alone,
He felt perfectly well.

O
Open-mouthed oyster!

15b. O was once a little owl,
Owly,
Prowly,
Howly,
Owly,
Browny fowly,
Little owl!

15d. O was an owl who flew
All in the dark away;
Papa said, "What an owl you are!
Why don't you fly by day?"

P

16a. P was a pig
Who was not very big;
But his tail was too curly,
And that made him surly.

p
Cross little pig!

16c. P was a polly,
All red, blue and green –
The most beautiful polly
That ever was seen.

p
Poor little polly!

16b. P was once a little pump,
Pumpy,
Slumpy,
Flumpy,
Pumpy,
Dumpy, thumpy,
Little pump!

16d. P was a little pig,
Went out to take a walk;
Papa, he said, "If piggy dead,
He'd all turn into pork!"

Q

17a. Q was a quail
With a very short tail,
And he fed upon corn
In the evening and morn.

q
Quaint little quail!

17c. Q was a quill
Made into a pen;
But I do not know where,
And I cannot say when.

q
Nice little quill!

17b. Q was once a little quail,
Quaily,
Faily,
Daily,
Quaily,
Stumpy-taily,
Little quail!

17d. Q was a quince that hung
Upon a garden tree;
Papa, he brought it with him home
And ate it with his tea.

R

18a. R was a rabbit
Who had a bad habit
Of eating the flowers
In gardens and bowers.

r
Naughty fat rabbit!

18c. R was a rattlesnake,
Rolled up so tight,
Those who saw him ran quickly
For fear he should bite.

r
Rattlesnake bite!

18b. R was once a little rose,
Rosy,
Posy,
Nosy,
Rosy,
Blowsy, growsy,
Little rose!

18d. R was a railway rug
Extremely large and warm;
Papa, he wrapped it round his hea
In a most dreadful storm.

S

19a. S was the sugar-tongs,
Nippity-nee,
To take up the sugar
To put in our tea.

S
Nippity-nee!

19c. S was a screw,
To screw down a box;
And then it was fastened
Without any locks.

S
Valuable screw!

19b. S was once a little shrimp,
Shrimpy,
Nimpy,
Flimpy,
Shrimpy,
Jumpy, jimpy,
Little shrimp!

19d. S was Papa's new stick,
Papa's new thumping stick,
To thump extremely wicked boys,
Because it was so thick.

T

20a. T was a tortoise
All yellow and black:
He walked slowly away,
And he never came back.

t

Torty never came back!

20b. T was once a little thrush,
  Thrushy,
  Hushy,
  Bushy,
  Thrushy,
 Flitty, flushy,
 Little thrush!

20c. T was a thimble,
Of silver so bright!
When placed on the finger,
It fitted so tight!

t

Nice little thimble!

20d. T was a tumbler full
 of punch all hot and good;
Papa, he drank it up, when in
 The middle of a wood.

U

21a. U was an urn
All polished and bright,
And full of hot water
At noon and at night.

u
Useful old urn!

21c. U was an upper coat,
Woolly and warm,
To wear over all
In the snow of the storm.

u
What a nice upper coat!

21b. U was once a little urn,
Urny,
Burny,
Turny,
Urny,
Bubbly, burny,
Little urn!

21d. U was a silver urn
Full of hot scalding water;
Papa said, "If that urn were mine,
I'd give it to my daughter!"

V

22a. V was a villa
Which stood on a hill,
By the side of a river
And close to a mill.

V
Nice little villa!

22c. V was a veil
With a border upon it
And a ribbon to tie it
All round a pink bonnet.

V
Pretty green veil!

22b. V was once a little vine,
Viny,
Winy,
Twiny,
Viny,
Twisty-twiny,
Little vine!

22d. V was a villain – once
He stole a piece of beef.
Papa, he said, "Oh, dreadful man
That villain is a thief!"

W

23a. **W** was a whale
With a very long tail,
Whose movements were frantic
Across the Atlantic.

W
Monstrous old whale!

23c. **W** was a watch,
Where, in letters of gold,
The hour of the day
You might always behold.

W
Beautiful watch!

23b. **W** was once a whale,
Whaly,
Scaly,
Shaly,
Whaly,
Tumbly-taily,
Mighty whale!

23d. **W** was a watch of gold:
It told the time of day,
So that Papa knew when to come
And when to go away.

X

24a. X was King Xerxes,
Who, more than all Turks, is
Renowned for his fashion
Of fury and passion.

X
Angry old Xerxes!

24c. X was King Xerxes,
Who wore on his head
A mighty large turban,
Green, yellow and red.

X
Look at King Xerxes!

24b. X was once the great King Xerxes,
Xerxy,
Perxy,
Turxy,
Xerxy,
Linxy, lurxy,
Great King Xerxes!

24d. X was King Xerxes, whom
Papa much wished to know;
But this he could not do, becau
Xerxes died long ago.

Y

25a. Y was a yew
Which flourished and grew
By a quiet abode
Near the side of a road.

y
Dark little yew!

25c. Y was a yak
From the land of Tibet;
Except his white tail,
He was all black as jet.

y
Look at the yak!

25b. Y was once a little yew,
Yedwy,
Fewdy,
Crudy,
Yewdy,
Growdy, grewdy,
Little yew!

25d. Y was a youth who kicked
And screamed and cried like mad;
Papa, he said, "Your conduct is
Abominably bad!"

Z

26a. Z was some zinc,
So shiny and bright,
Which caused you to wink
In the sun's merry light.

Z
Beautiful zinc!

26c. Z was a zebra,
All striped white and black –
And if he were tame,
You might ride on his back.

Z
Pretty striped zebra!

26b. Z was once a piece of zinc,
Tinky,
Winky,
Blinky,
Tinky,
Tinkly minky,
Piece of zinc!

26d. Z was a zebra striped
And streaked with lines of black
Papa said once, he thought he'd like
A ride upon his back.

1e.   A tumbled down and hurt his Arm against a bit of wood.

2e.   B said, "My Boy, oh, do not cry – it cannot do you good!"

3e.   C said, "A Cup of coffee hot can't do you any harm."

4e.   D said, "A Doctor should be fetched, and he would cure the arm."

5e.   E said, "An Egg beat up with milk would quickly make him well."

6e.   F said, "A Fish, if broiled, might cure, if only by the smell."

7e.   G said, "Green Gooseberry fool, the best of cures I hold."

8e.   H said, "His Hat should be kept on, to keep him from the cold."

9e.   I said, "Some Ice upon his head will make him better soon."

10e.   J said, "Some Jam, if spread on bread, or given in a spoon!"

11e.   K said, "A Kangaroo is here – this picture let him see."

12e.   L said, "A Lamp pray keep alight, to make some barley tea."

13e.   M said, "A Mulberry or two might give him satisfaction."

14e.   N said, "Some Nuts, if rolled about, might be a slight attraction."

15e.   O said, "An Owl might make him laugh, if only it would wink."

16e.   P said, "Some Poetry might be read aloud, to make him think."

17e.   Q said, "A Quince I recommend – a Quince, or else a Quail."

18e.   R said, "Some Rats might make him move, if fastened by their tail."

19e.   S said, "A Song should now be sung, in hopes to make him laugh!"

20e.   T said, "A Turnip might avail, if sliced or cut in half!"

21e.   U said, "An Urn, with water hot, place underneath his chin!"

22e.   V said, "I'll stand upon a chair and play a Violin!"

23e.   W said, "Some Whisky-Whizgigs fetch, some marbles and a ball!"

24e.   X said, "Some double-XX ale would be the best of all!"

25e.   Y said, "Some Yeast mixed up with salt would make a perfect plaster!"

26e.   Z said, "Here is a box of Zinc! Get in, my little master!

      We'll shut you up! We'll nail you down! We will, my little master!

      We think we've all heard quite enough of this your sad disaster!"

EDITIONS OF EDWARD LEAR'S WORKS

BN1   *A Book of Nonsense* (London: Thomas McLean, 1846)

BN2   *A Book of Nonsense*, 2nd Edn (London: Thomas McLean, 1856?)

BN3   *A Book of Nonsense*, 3rd Edn (London: Routledge, Warne and Routledge, 1861)

LL   *Laughable Lyrics: A Fourth Book of Nonsense Poems, Songs, Botany, Music, Etc.* (London: Robert John Bush, 1877)

MN   *More Nonsense, Pictures, Rhymes, Botany, Etc.* (London: Robert John Bush, 1872)

NS   *Nonsense Songs, Stories, Botany and Alphabets* (London: Robert John Bush, 1871)

NOTE ON THE TEXTS

This volume collects the four books of "nonsense" published by Lear during his lifetime. In the interest of an improved reading experience, the material has been rearranged wherever appropriate and convenient. For publication details of the individual books, see the notes to the relevant sections below. Spelling and punctuation have been standardized, modernized and made consistent throughout.

NOTES

A BOOK OF NONSENSE

Lear's first book of nonsense poetry was published in two volumes in February 1846 (BN1) and reprinted in one volume in 1855 or 1856 (BN2). The first two editions, both published anonymously at Lear's own expense, comprise seventy-two illustrated limericks in addition to the one on the title page ('Old Derry down Derry'). In the first edition, the verses are arranged over three lines; in the second, over five. The much enlarged third edition (BN3) – published in December 1861 – includes 112 illustrated limericks; three of the original rhymes and their drawings (Nos. 113–15 in the present volume) do not appear in BN3 or later editions, where the limericks are again laid out over three lines. We follow the text, the illustrations and the order of BN3 (the sheets of BN1 and BN2 were not bound in a consistent order). Some of the drawings are taken from BN1 and BN2 for better quality. The forty-three new limericks that appeared in BN3 and later editions are marked with an asterisk.

TITLE PAGE, *Derry down Derry*: A meaningless expression often used as a filler line in traditional folk songs, and the name of a character from the mummers' plays.

DEDICATION, *Edward, 13th Earl of Derby*: Edward Smith-Stanley, 13th Earl of Derby (1775–1851).

11. l.2. *sarpint*: Serpent.

NONSENSE SONGS AND STORIES

The nonsense songs and stories in this section are taken from NS, which also included 'Nonsense Cookery' (see pp. 225–27), the first series of 'Nonsense Botany' (1.1–1.10; see pp. 229–31) and the first three series of 'Nonsense Alphabets' (1a–26a, 1b–26b and 1c–26c; see pp. 241–66). We follow the order of the original volume, although some of the drawings have been moved to better suit the text flow.

MR AN5 MRS SPIKKY SPARROW, l. 57. *the Monument*: The Monument to the Great Fire of London, constructed between 1671 and 1677.

MORE NONSENSE

All the material in this section is taken from MN, which also includes the second series of 'Nonsense Botany' (2.1–2.12; see pp. 232–34). We have decided to keep the 'Twenty-Six Nonsense Rhymes and Pictures' as a separate sub-section rather than group it with the other five alphabet series (pp. 241–67). The texts and the drawings follow the order of the original volume. The limericks have been laid out over five lines rather than four, as they appear in MN.

INTRODUCTION, last line. *Messrs Routledge and Warne… published in 1861*: The date has been corrected from "1843" in MN, an obvious mistake. Lear had probably written, or meant, "1863" (the date stated in an 'Advertisement' in LL). BN3 had in fact been published in December 1861 (despite its dedication being dated "London, 1862"). Lear sold the rights in his *Book of Nonsense* to his new publishers in November 1862 for a flat fee of £200.

ONE HUNDRED NONSENSE PICTURES AND RHYMES, 53. l. 1. *man*: changed from "person" in MN; 58. l. 4. *daffydowndillies*: daffodils.

TWENTY-SIX NONSENSE RHYMES AND PICTURES, 24. l. 1. *double-extra-XX*: During the nineteenth century, breweries produced a number of ales designated by X marks, the weakest being X and the strongest XXXX; 25. l. 1. *The Yonghy-Bonghy-Bò*: See the poem 'The Courtship of the Yonghy-Bonghy-Bò' in LL, pp. 201–5.

LAUGHABLE LYRICS

Lear's fourth and final book of nonsense poetry (LL) contains, in addition to the ten 'Laughable Lyrics', the third series of 'Nonsense Botany' (3.1–3.10; see pp. 235–37) and two further series of 'Nonsense Alphabets' (1d–26d and 1e–26e; see pp. 241–67).

THE DONG WITH A LUMINOUS NOSE, l. 30. *For the Jumblies came in a sieve, they did*: See the song 'The Jumblies', pp. 77–80.

THE PELICAN CHORUS, note. *Professor Pomè*: The Italian conductor and composer Alessandro Pomè (1851–1934).

THE COURTSHIP OF THE YONGHY-BONGHY-BÒ, l. 71. *a hoddy-doddy*: A short and dumpy person.

THE NEW VESTMENTS, l. 28. *prigged*: Stole.

THE QUANGLE-WANGLE'S HAT: For the Quangle-Wangle, see also 'The Story of the Four Little Children Who Went Round the World', pp. 95–105.

THE CUMMERBUND, title: A cummerbund is a sash or girdle worn around the waist; l. 1. *dobie*: A dhoby, an Indian washerman or washerwoman; l. 3. *punkahs*: Large hand-held fans; l. 6. *kamsamahs*: Table attendants; butlers; l. 7. *kitmutgars*: Male servants waiting at table; l. 8. *tchokis*: Chairs; l. 11. *chuprassies*: Attendants occupying an important position in the households of Indian landowners; l. 14. *ayahs*: Nurses or maidservants; l. 15. *mussak*: A leather water bag (normally spelt "mussuck"); l. 17. *nullahs*: Watercourses; l. 19. *goreewallahs*: Coachmen; l. 21. *bheesties*: Servants who supply an establishment with water; l. 23. *jampan*: A kind of sedan chair carried by four men; l. 26. *nimmak*: Salt.

THE AKOND OF SWAT, title: The poem was inspired by a short piece that appeared in the *Times of India* on 18th July 1873:

> It is reported from Swat that the Akhoond's son has quarrelled with his father, and left the parental presence with a following of 500 sowars, refusing to listen to the Akhoond's orders to come back.

An "akhoond" is a religious leader, teacher or scholar. "Sowars" are mounted attendants. Swat is a district in northern Pakistan, around 200 km north-west of Islamabad. In Lear's time, it was part of British India; l. 19. GARROTTE: Throttle (in order to rob a person); l. 29. SHALOTT: A reference to the famous poem 'The Lady of Shalott' by Alfred, Lord Tennyson (1809–92).

NONSENSE COOKERY, BOTANY AND ALPHABETS

The material in this section is taken from NS, MN and LL. 'Nonsense Cookery', the first series of 'Nonsense Botany' (1.1–1.10) and the first three series of 'Nonsense Alphabets' (1a–26a, 1b–26b and 1c–26c) are reproduced from NS; the second series of 'Nonsense Botany' (2.1–2.12) is taken from MN; the third series of 'Nonsense Botany' (3.1–3.10) and the last two series of 'Nonsense Alphabets' (1d–26d and 1e–26e) are reprinted from LL.

NONSENSE ALPHABETS, 24b. l. 1. *the*: Changed from "a" in NS.

FURTHER NONSENSE

If you would like to expand your knowledge of Lear's artistry beyond the four books he published in his lifetime, there are a number of volumes you can find online or in bookshops. *Queery Leary Nonsense* (London: Mills & Boon, 1911) is a posthumous collection of unpublished Lear works compiled by Lady Strachey. It includes humorous drawings, letters, nonsense sketches and verses, and a colour reproduction of 'The Bird Book'. In 1926 Frederick Warne published, in a limited edition of 1,000 copies, a *Facsimile of a Nonsense Alphabet* drawn and written by Edward Lear, containing an unpublished pictorial A–Z. Another rediscovered nonsense alphabet was published by Doubleday in 1952.

The Complete Nonsense and Other Verse (London: Penguin, 2006), compiled and edited with an introduction and notes by Vivien Noakes, includes most of Lear's published and unpublished poetical works, accompanied by their illustrations. Although the reproduction quality of some of the drawings is poor and the integrity of the original published collections has been destroyed, leading to a bewildering, fragmented reading experience, this remains a useful single-volume reference tool covering Lear's entire oeuvre.

BIOGRAPHICAL NOTE

Edward Lear was born in Upper Holloway, London, in 1812, the twentieth of twenty-one children. With financial difficulties plaguing his father, the young Edward was placed in the charge of his eldest sister, Ann, who was responsible for his upbringing. He attended school for a brief period, but he was mostly educated at home by Ann and another sister, Sarah. This lack of formal education may have been the result of continuous ill health, with Edward suffering from asthma, bronchitis and epilepsy. It was his sisters who instructed him in the art of drawing and painting, and, from the age of fifteen, such work was to earn him his living.

By 1829 he had become an ornithological draughtsman, serving an apprenticeship of sorts under the famed Prideaux John Selby (1788–1867). Following the opening of the Zoological Gardens in London in 1829, Lear was granted permission to make drawings of the parrots.

This led to the publication in 1832 of Lear's *Illustrations of the Family of Psittacidæ, or Parrots*. Over the next few years he contributed to works by Selby and Sir William Jardine (1800–74), among others, forging a reputation as one of the country's foremost avian illustrators. Lord Stanley, the 13th Earl of Derby, was one of his admirers, and saw Lear as just the artist he needed to produce an accurate record of the menagerie he had been building at his home at Knowsley, near Liverpool. Between 1831 and 1837, Lear spent large periods of time at Knowsley, making drawings and watercolours of the birds and beasts that dwelt there.

The large country house, "where children and mirth abounded", as Lear later recalled, was also the setting for the drawing and penning of much of the material for *A Book of Nonsense*.

In 1837, with Lear's poor eyesight deteriorating further and the climate of northern England exacerbating his bronchitis and asthma, Lord Stanley offered to send him to Rome, in the hope that the climate would prove more congenial to his health.

Landscape work had by now taken the place of natural history for Lear. His travels around Italy produced *Views in Rome and Its Environs* in 1841 and *Illustrated Excursions in Italy* in 1846. Queen Victoria was so impressed with the latter that she asked Lear to give her twelve drawing lessons. 1846 also saw the publication of *A Book of Nonsense*, a collection of nonsense verse and accompanying drawings. It was published to little fanfare, yet the revised third edition, published in 1861, proved an enormous success and brought what we now know as the "limerick" – the term is a late-nineteenth-century coinage – into the public consciousness. Twenty-four editions followed in Lear's lifetime alone, and the book has never been out of print since.

Lear continued to live an itinerant artist's life, with years spent travelling through Greece and the Greek islands. It was in 1867, when the poet John Addington Symonds's daughter Janet was ill and confined to her bed, that Lear wrote for her 'The Owl and the Pussy Cat', which was later published in *Nonsense Songs, Stories, Botany and Alphabets* (1871) and became one of the most enduringly popular poems written in the English language. Two more collections of illustrated nonsense poetry – *More Nonsense* and *Laughable Lyrics* – followed in 1872 and 1877, respectively, cementing Lear's reputation as one of the most original poets who ever lived.

Edward Lear died of heart disease in 1888 at his villa in Sanremo. His achievements as a painter were overlooked for many years due to his enormous success as a writer of humorous verse. Throughout the twentieth century, however, this lopsided view began to be redressed, and he is now recognized as a skilled and powerful landscape artist, as well as a towering figure in ornithological drawing and the nation's favourite "nonsense" writer.

INDEX OF TITLES AND FIRST LINES

Titles of poems are in italics. The notation appended in brackets to each entry indicates the collection or series it is taken from:

BN: *A Book of Nonsense*
MN: *More Nonsense Poetry*
NA1: First series of 'Nonsense Alphabets'
NA2: Second series of 'Nonsense Alphabets'
NA3: Third series of 'Nonsense Alphabets'
NA4: Fourth series of 'Nonsense Alphabets'
NA5: Fifth series of 'Nonsense Alphabets'
NB1: First series of 'Nonsense Botany'
NB2: Second series of 'Nonsense Botany'
NB3: Third series of 'Nonsense Botany'
NRP: 'Nonsense Rhymes and Pictures'

NONSENSE ALPHABETS

NONSENSE BOTANY

NONSENSE RHYMES (LIMERICKS)

NONSENSE SONGS AND LYRICS